Swansea Psychiatric Education Centre
01792-516568

This book is due for return on or before the last date shown below.

THE HEALTH DEBATE LIVE: 45 INTERVIEWS FOR "LEADING FOR HEALTH"

THE HEALTH DEBATE LIVE:
45 INTERVIEWS FOR
"LEADING FOR HEALTH"

Interviews by
ANDREW VALLANCE OWEN,
Secretary of the BMA's working party

Published by the British Medical Journal
Tavistock Square, London WC1H 9JR

© British Medical Journal 1992

First published 1992

British Library Cataloguing in Publication Data

Health Debate Live: 45 Interviews for
Leading for Health
I. Smith, Richard
362.10941

ISBN 0-7279-0740-9

Typeset by Cambridge Composing (UK) Ltd
Printed and bound in Great Britain by
Latimer Trend & Company Ltd, Plymouth

Contents

Page

Introduction   xi
    RICHARD SMITH, *editor, British Medical Journal*

PUBLIC AND OCCUPATIONAL HEALTH

Need for sensible research   3
    NICK BLACK, *senior lecturer in public health medicine,*
    Health Services Research Unit, London School of Hygiene
    and Tropical Medicine

Inequalities in health: ready for action   7
    WALTER HOLLAND, *professor, Department of Public Health*
    Medicine, United Medical and Dental Schools of Guy's and
    St Thomas's Hospitals

Health as a broader issue   11
    ALEX SCOTT-SAMUEL, *chair, Public Health Alliance*

Health promotion: planning in Wales   14
    JOHN CATFORD, *executive director, Health Promotion*
    Authority for Wales

Funding for needs   18
    EILEEN WAIN, *chairman, BMA's Committee for Public*
    Health Medicine and Community Health

CONTENTS

Need for more expenditure on health and safety   23
    JOE KEARNS, *former chairman, BMA's Occupational*
    Health Committee, and chairman, European Communities
    Committee

PATIENTS, PRIMARY CARE, AND THE COMMUNITY

Patient's rights and participation in health care policy   29
    LINDA LAMONT, *director, Patients Association*

Waiting lists: keeping patients informed   32
    MARIANNE RIGGE, *director, College of Health*

The need for a flexible approach   35
    JULIAN TUDOR HART, *general practitioner, West*
    Glamorgan, and Department of General Practice, St Mary's
    Hospital, London

Competition among providers   38
    MICHAEL GOLDSMITH, *former general practitioner trainer,*
    director, Medisure, and research fellow, Centre for Policy
    Studies

The role of community health councils   42
    TOBY HARRIS, *director, Association of Community Health*
    Councils of England and Wales

Funding and deprived areas   45
    ROS LEVENSON, *director, Greater London Association of*
    Community Health Councils

SECONDARY CARE AND EDUCATION

Teamwork and collaboration   51
    STEPHEN HUNTER, *consultant in psychological medicine,*
    University Hospital of Wales, Cardiff, and former
    chairman, BMA's Junior Doctors Committee

Breaking down the divide   55
SIR DILLWYN WILLIAMS, *former chairman, Conference of*
Medical Royal Colleges

Quality standards, costings, and the London problem   58
CYRIL CHANTLER, *clinical dean, United Medical and*
Dental Schools of Guy's and St Thomas's Hospitals

Matching resources with needs   63
HARRY KEEN, *chairman, NHS Support Federation*

Being prepared and the value of non-clinical audit   65
BRENDAN DEVLIN, *secretary, National Confidential*
Enquiry into Perioperative Deaths

Mental health   68
JIM BIRLEY, *consultant psychiatrist, Bethlem Royal and*
Maudsley Hospitals, London

Management at arm's length   71
PADDY ROSS, *chairman, BMA's Joint Consultants*
Committee

Consultants' performance and counterproductive incentives   76
JOHN CHAWNER, *chairman, BMA's Central Consultants*
and Specialists Committee

Payments for skills and extra work   81
LORD IAN MCCOLL, *professor of surgery, United Medical*
and Dental Schools of Guy's and St Thomas's Hospitals

A call for definitions   84
W M ROSS, *secretary, Conference of Colleges, Royal*
College of Radiologists

Cost consciousness and failure of the advisory structure   87
ANGUS FORD, *chairman, BMA's Scottish Council*

Need for more information technology   91
RUSSELL HOPKINS, *chairman, BMA's Welsh Council Unit,
and former general manager, University Hospital of Wales,
Cardiff*

Time for management   95
JOHN HALLIDAY, *former chairman, BMA's Northern
Ireland Council*

Rethinking education   98
ELIZABETH SHORE, *dean of postgraduate medical education,
North West Thames Regional Health Authority*

The need for an academic training   101
COLIN SMITH, *chairman, BMA's Medical Academic Staff
Committee*

POLITICS AND MANAGEMENT

Offering an alternative   109
SAM GALBRAITH MP, *Labour Scottish Spokesman on
Health*

Ringfencing for the disadvantaged   114
NICHOLAS WINTERTON MP, *chairman, House of Commons
Health Service Select Committee*

A call for continued pressure on funding   117
RENEE SHORT, *former chairman, House of Commons Social
Services Select Committee*

A regional approach to health   120
GREG PARSTON, *executive director, Office for Public
Management*

Soft approaches and changing roles   125
PAMELA CHARLWOOD, *director, and* STEPHEN HALPERN,
*project development manager, Institute for Health Services
Management*

The increasing power of the consumer   129
    BRIAN EDWARDS, *regional general manager, Trent Regional*
    Health Authority

Purchasing primary care   133
    MICHAEL O'BRIEN, *director of public health, East Anglia*
    Regional Health Authority

District health authorities and need for credibility with
consultants   136
    JACK HOWELL, *chairman, Southampton and South West*
    Hampshire District Health Authority

Self governing trust: a stable first year   139
    MAURICE BURROWS, *former chairman, Wirral Health*
    Authority, and chairman, Wirral Hospital Trust

HEALTH POLICY AND ECONOMICS

Roles, models, and lack of government imagination   145
    DAVID J HUNTER, *director, Nuffield Institute for Health*
    Studies, University of Leeds

An unfinished story   150
    RUDOLF KLEIN, *professor, Centre for the Analysis of Social*
    Policy, University of Bath

Working towards large health benefits   154
    CHARLES NORMAND, *professor of health policy, London*
    School of Hygiene and Tropical Medicine

Towards effective health care   157
    IAN RUSSELL, *director, Health Services Research Unit,*
    University of Aberdeen

Resource management: need for a definition   161
    MARTIN BUXTON, *professor, Health Economics Research*
    Group, Brunel University

CONTENTS

An insurance based system   165
DAVID GREEN, *director, Health and Welfare Unit, Institute of Economic Affairs, London*

Putting a better case to the Treasury   168
ALAN MAYNARD, *professor, Centre for Health Economics, University of York*

More choices for patients   172
ROBERT MAXWELL, *chief executive, King's Fund*

An American perspective   176
DONALD W LIGHT, *professor of health services and policy, University of Medicine and Dentistry of New Jersey*

Introduction

Reading the interviews with a wide range of people for the BMA's document *Leading for Health*, I came away with the impression that they constituted the health debate that we are not having. So much of the current debate over health and health care is superficial and conducted as in a pantomime — "Yes you did, no we didn't." Public debate is restricted by people striking poses and sticking to them regardless of evidence or sneaking doubts they may be wrong. These interviews are rough and ready in their structure, but the untidiness reflects people thinking out loud about what will be the key issues in health into the next century.

Some of those who supported the idea that the BMA produce a manifesto for health may have imagined that the small working group would quickly hammer out a new and coherent policy for the association. It soon became apparent that that was impossible: the time was too short and the issues too complex. Instead, the group tried to identify what would be the central unresolved questions. One way that it did this was to draw up a list of key participants in the health debate and interview them. The interviews published in this book are the result.

People were selected because they are widely respected, were expected to have something useful and important to say, and reflected a wide range of opinions and disciplines. Not all of the major players were interviewed, and the most conspicuous absentees are the health spokespeople of the major parties. We thought that they — particularly in the run up to a general election — would find it difficult to talk openly and broadly. Once selected, the people were interviewed by Dr Andrew Vallance-Owen, the secretary of the working party. Dr Vallance-Owen encouraged the interviewees to talk broadly and candidly, and he afterwards prepared an account of the interview. The interviews published here have deliberately been only lightly edited, and all of the participants have approved the accounts of their own interviews.

When first approached, all of those interviewed were offered confidentiality. The interviews were read only by the six people on the working party. But because so many interesting points were thrown up by the interviews we thought that they merited publication. It would have been a shame to waste so much original thought, time, and effort. Consequently we offered the interviewees the chance to have their interview published, and most accepted. A few understandably declined. We encouraged people not to rewrite their interviews because we wanted to preserve the candour — albeit at the cost of neat phrasing.

Because most interviewees ranged over a wide range of subjects we have not attempted to group the interviews by subject. Rather we have grouped the interviewees by their background; but hospital doctors talk about primary care, health economists discuss structures in the care services, and managers consider preventive medicine. The idea was to open up the debate not restrict it.

Several themes emerge repeatedly in the interviews, and these were picked up in the final report, which was sent to all members of the BMA and widely distributed among politicians and opinion formers in health. The report asks a great many questions and suggests that most have been inadequately answered by all the political parties and by health policy experts.

The need for a strategy for health, the health and community care services, and the educational and research endeavours that underpin them is one of the central questions raised by the report and by many of the interviewees. After years of havering there seems now to be consensus that a strategy is needed but much less agreement on how the strategy should be formed and evaluated and how the strategies for the care services should be fitted together with those for health and for education and research. At the moment there are more strategies than coherent connections.

Funding of services inevitably comes up time and time again in the interviews. People think out loud about different ways of funding the health service, although no major political party is currently considering any option apart from funding most of health care from direct taxation. Still more difficult than the question of how to fund health and community care is how much to spend. Health economists have theoretical answers, but these are annoyingly unhelpful in the real world. Most difficult of all is the question of how to allocate resources among services, treatments, and patients. The word rationing with its emotive overtones is commonly used in these circumstances — and is used by many of the interviewees — but it may be better to talk of resource allocation, emphasising less the element of denial and more the element of choice. Questions then arise on who should make these decisions and how they should be made. How much, for instance, should the public be involved in allocating resources? The interviewees have different views.

Much of the book is devoted to the separation of purchasers and providers, an idea that was at the centre of the government's reforms of the NHS. Most of the interviewees accept this idea, and much of the debate is over who should be the purchasers — fundholding general practitioners, district health authorities, family health services authorities, or purchasing consortia — and how should the providers be organised. The book shows a wide range of views on this central issue.

Research, education, audit, and attempts to improve quality arise frequently in the book as do the links between them. These in the end may be much more important drivers of how health care develops than how the health service is structured. Many of the interviewees are much concerned about the quality of education and research in Britain, and they are worried that audit may give rise to more jargon and activity than change.

Many of those interviewed are managers or health professionals with an interest in management, and numerous ideas are expressed on how management in the health service can be developed. In particular, there is broad agreement on the need for better and more relevant information within the health service but also a fear that resources may be wasted in collecting information that will be of little use in improving the care of patients.

Finally, manpower crops up regularly in the interviews. Health and community care is ultimately about people caring for other people, which is why the biggest proportion of the expenditure is on salaries. Yet in both sectors use of what the Americans call human resources has been poor. Many sections of the workforce are poorly paid; many — most famously junior doctors — are over-worked; career development is poorly planned; morale is low; sickness rates are high; and occupational health services are rudimentary. These are serious problems for organisations that depend so much on people, and the interviewees look at the problems and consider some answers.

In the end this is not a book that proposes neat answers for readily identified problems. Rather it captures an important debate — a debate that is happening in all countries — at an early stage.

RICHARD SMITH
Editor, British Medical Journal

PUBLIC AND OCCUPATIONAL HEALTH

Need for sensible research

NICK BLACK, *senior lecturer in public health medicine, Health Services Research Unit, London School of Hygiene and Tropical Medicine*

Research

Needs

Assessing patients' needs will be crucial not only in relation to funding and allocation but also to research. Occasionally there is an unmet need but no effective treatment (for example, in patients with senile dementia), so if the need can be clearly demonstrated then research in that area should be a priority. How much money is being wasted on treatment of doubtful effectiveness? There must be more research on effectiveness and outcomes, taking into account patients' views.

There is a need for a national research and development strategy. Not enough is spent on health services research and what money is spent is not always spent in the best way. There are many independent small, poorly designed studies. Studies could be better organised and coordinated to produce a much improved product.

I believe that Professor Michael Peckham, the new director of research and development, is trying to adopt a serious strategy, and it would be good if he could achieve the target of 1.5% of the health spending budget to be spent on research and development. One problem, however, is that regional finance directors are saying that postgraduate training should be included in the 1.5% — this will enable them to reach the target easily. I think that the research and development budget should not include training, but, apart from that, the strategy should lead to better quality research and, hopefully, better priorities for research being set. The research community must be involved in setting this agenda.

There is a need for research related to clinical practice, particularly in relation to decisions which will have to be made by

3

purchasers. For instance, how many transurethral prostatectomies should health authorities plan to buy for their local population? What are the appropriate indications? There is great variation from area to area, but how many prostatectomies should urologists be doing? Diabetes seems well researched in theory but is still a difficult subject in practice; there is a lack of clear scientific information on indications for treatment and on the prevalence in the community. In many clinical subjects there are real problems with the lack of local and research based data.

Dissemination of information

The United States have introduced patient outcome research teams (PORTs). The first three were set up two years ago; there are now 10. These are each funded to the tune of $1m a year for five years and look at one or two specific conditions — for example, benign prostatic hyperplasia or carcinoma of the prostate. One of the problems is that if research is not related to a PORT project then it is difficult to get money for it. Critics have also suggested that the $5m for each project might be better spent on examining possibilities for how to disseminate clinical information to doctors at large and how to bring about real changes in medical practice.

I believe that dissemination of information may best be achieved through avenues such as editorials in medical journals written by influential doctors. Medical audit within a hospital will not be enough in itself. We also need comparative audit between hospitals, which would encourage the injection of new ideas. If the profession adopts the view that there are just a few "bad apples" around then this will lead to cosy complacency. All doctors must look critically at what they are doing in relation to their peers.

Patient input

There must be patient (consumer) input into research on outcomes and effectiveness so that quality of life measures can be included alongside so called objective biological measures. Patients are happy to supply information through questionnaires and surveys, which are generally not expensive. There is a particular need to involve lay people in health services research areas such as maternity care — Iain Chalmers at Oxford has tried to do this.

4

Purchaser-provider concept

I believe that the purchaser-provider system is here to stay. I see practical problems with general practitioner fundholding. The power shift to general practitioners is fine if the right information is provided to practitioners and to patients; otherwise the providers will call the tune.

One of the problems is that the bulk of hospital admissions is demand led — that is, accident and emergency admissions; most medical, obstetric, and psychiatric admissions; and a half of surgical admissions. Therefore, if the system stays as it is at present general practitioner fundholders will continue to have little real discretion and most contracting will be left to the district health authority.

If the market is to work it must be sophisticated. Contracts are generally poor on detail and have very few quality parameters. If the market is to be run properly it will cost a great deal of money to provide the necessary information systems and the people to run them. The information technology costs alone could run to £2-3bn nationally. This would, of course, increase the percentage of the gross domestic product spent on health, but who is to audit the value of information technology for patient care? A key project for the Audit Commission should be to look at information technology and administrative staff in the coming years before developing the reforms further. There is a need to be convinced that the expense of generating the required cost data will be justified by improvement in the efficiency of the NHS.

Manpower

I strongly believe that staffing in the health service will be a key issue in the '90s. How can we continue to strive for high quality and better standards with a tight policy of cost containment? There needs to be a complete review of the roles of different health professionals — boundaries may have to be redefined and different types of staff substituted for some work. This type of review in itself will have to lead to a complete rethink of training needs.

I believe that the United Kingdom might have 50% more district general hospitals than it needs and can afford to staff. What is the right level of core service to be provided by a district general hospital and what is the right level of staffing? I have looked at 31 district general hospitals in three health regions and have found a fourfold variation in nursing staff levels and a threefold variation in junior doctor levels, having taken case mix into account. We should have a real acute service in larger district hospitals and preserve small community hospitals as the quid pro quo. We must also look at better usage of hospital facilities. It is crazy that highly expensive CAT scanners are used for only six hours a day and that outpatient departments close down at 5 pm, when people are just coming home from work.

I am concerned about the threat of a loss of pay parity for clinical academic staff. If not resolved I believe that, in the course of time, clinical academics will have much less motivation to fulfil a service commitment.

In the NHS we are already seeing decreased cooperation from consultants in relation to research work — for instance, one self governing trust is asking who will pay for the extra outpatient visit required for the follow up of patients in one particular current study. If clinicians will not give their time to enable the collection of data on effectiveness of treatments then the cost of research will rise dramatically. Michael Peckham will have to tackle this and the issue has to be put on the NHS Management Executive's agenda.

Conclusion

Changes in research funding over the next two years, with the responsibility for the cost of the research infrastructure being moved to the research councils, will need to be carefully monitored and the type of projects being funded reviewed to ensure sensible balance and spread.

Inequalities in health: ready for action

WALTER HOLLAND, *professor, Department of Public Health Medicine, United Medical and Dental Schools of Guy's and St Thomas's Hospitals*

Assessment of need

A great deal of work was done on needs assessment under the auspices of the Department of Health in the late '60s directed by the first chief scientist, D R Cohen — in particular the *Portfolio for Health,*[1] but also a wealth of other material (over 100 references). I was horrified to hear recently that the medical side of the department knew little of this work.

All research in this area has now been stopped at St Thomas's Hospital. It opened a Pandora's box, but I am doubtful whether it was a profitable area of inquiry, mainly because even when need was clearly demonstrated there were no clearer criteria as to what was going to be treated, how effective the treatment would be, and what priority it would be given.

There will always be variations from one district to another, but for most districts there is already an adequate knowledge of the prevalence (if not incidence) of many conditions. Therefore, most district health authorities should be able to assess the number of people with specific conditions by extrapolating from published information and by using age, sex, social class, and ethnic registers.

There is somewhat less information on conditions such as hernia and osteoarthritis, so these *do* need epidemiological studies on prevalence. There seem, however, to be no funds for such studies anywhere in the NHS. I accept that some work is being done with the department under Project 26, but I believe these studies are superficial in not tackling outcomes or variations with different procedures.

I therefore believe that the current concentration on health needs assessment is nonsense. Unmet needs will always be discovered, but there is no point in discovering them if nothing is going to be done. As an example, the Royal College of Physicians and Nuffield Provincial Hospitals Trust and, separately, the Office of Population Censuses and Surveys did good studies on the need for disability services. In addition workers at St Thomas's Hospital have done two studies indicating the services required for those with disability. Next to no notice, however, has been taken of the work and the provision of services for disabled people is still very inadequate.

Inequities

Three main areas of inequity should be considered:

Inequity of outcome

As part of their European Community collaboration work our unit has compared avoidable death in a range of conditions over Europe.[2] In almost every condition in the United Kingdom the standardised mortality ratio has become worse from the 1970s to the 1980s.

In asthma the deterioration is mainly due to increased prevalence and incidence rather than increased diagnosis or ineffective treatment; more people need to be treated. In carcinoma of the cervix there are variations between health authorities (some of which have done their own internal inquiries); in some cases there have been failures of screening and in others failure of communication with patients. In some areas patients with hypertension have been diagnosed and referred at the right time, they have received the right initial treatment, but, instead of being referred back to general practice, have been followed up within the hospital, often by a succession of junior doctors, which has led to problems. In a final example the treatment of stroke has been considered; treatment leads to little change in standardised mortality ratios but preventive measures lead to significant improvement, particularly in district health authorities with poor populations and high levels of ethnic minorities.

These examples show that inequalities in outcome can be tackled now. For instance, in districts with high levels of ethnic minority groups priority should be given to controlling blood pressure in these groups. There must, however, be adequate information systems to undertake this sort of work.

Inequity of health status

The original Resource Allocation Working Party (RAWP) formula deliberately excluded social indices. As most of the differences in health status are due to social and environmental factors, adjusting by these factors could lead governments to spend money on health services rather than correcting the social and environmental inequalities. Spending money on health services is a cheap option and does nothing to correct the underlying causes. Thus in the original RAWP formula only health indices were used in order to make it clear to the government that it could not "escape" from its responsibility to correct the underlying factors. Now allocation is through weighted capitation, weighted 50% to standardised mortality ratio and 50% towards an index of deprivation based on demand on general practitioners. This is biased towards inadequacies in London rather than the north. This is an improvement but, if health is to improve, homelessness, diet, etc, in low income areas must be tackled.

Inequity of access

The RAWP formula was reasonably successful in allocating resources fairly to regions, but allocation to districts was less equitable. The new weighted capitation allocation would be much better for handing down funds to districts. But general practices, even of 9000-11 000 patients, are too small for sensible allocation of funds on an epidemiological basis.

I'm not sure what is a sensible size of population to be covered. For stability in relation to the number of cases arising and the contracting process a population of 0.25-0.5 million would be acceptable, preferably nearer 0.5 million. But if the population is too large the sensitivity to cope with specific local and social needs is lost — for example, targeting ethnic minorities for potential hypertension.

General considerations

I am generally concerned that there have been few, if any, clear decisions made through contracts on precisely what work is expected and at what levels of service. There needs to be a definition of a core service to be provided for all so that there can then be a discussion on what additional services are to be prioritised. This should include public discussion. The Oregon project is superficial and limited to Medicaid but has led to some degree of consensus. Whether this

9

will lead to a change in the American position, with half of health care expenditure being spent on the last six months of life, remains to be seen.

Prevention

The Health of the Nation is good in principle but concentrates on causes of death rather than causes of ill health.[3] A whole range of conditions which need to be considered include osteoarthritis, mental conditions, and disability. The report has stated that the government will concentrate only on things for which it has "measurable indices." There must also be a research strategy for studying other major causes of ill health and producing similar targets for the future.

Money and the patient

Money had been following the patient prior to the reforms, but extremely inadequately. To do the job properly the costings system used by the service has to be based on the individual patient, as originally suggested in *Accounting for Health*.[4] This would need individual patient NHS identity numbers to track costings and patients (with appropriate confidentiality), but, if the investment in the technology were made, it could lead to a significant reduction in contracting costs and the associated bureaucracy.

1 Nuffield Provincial Hospitals Trust. *Portfolio for health*. Vol 1 and 2. London: Oxford University Press, 1971 and 1973.
2 European Community. *Atlas of avoidable death*. 2nd ed. Vol 1. Oxford: Oxford University Press, 1991.
3 Secretary of State for Health. *The health of the nation*. London: HMSO, 1991. (Cm 1523.)
4 King's Fund. *Accounting for health*. London: King's fund, 1974.

Health as a broader issue

ALEX SCOTT-SAMUEL, *chair, Public Health Alliance*

Public health

I fully support the Public Health Alliance's document *Beyond Acheson — An Agenda for the New Public Health*.[1] I believe that the issue of health is now much wider than traditional health care and any discussion on health must include social issues such as poverty, unemployment, and housing. I'm sure that a million pounds would do more for health generally if spent on social security benefits, reducing income differentials, or instituting a national minimum wage.

There should be a proper department of "health" which includes both health care and the broad public health. This department would have prime responsibility for collaborating with all the other concerned government departments on health issues rather than taking them over. I think that the Department of Health is now slowly moving towards this type of approach with its publication of *The Health of the Nation*[2] but has not yet accepted that there are inequalities in health — it calls them "variations." Nevertheless, organisations should emphasise the whole question of inequalities and the health gains to be achieved from reducing them.

Incidentally, I'm also keen to see a health directorate to take forward health issues in the European Community. Currently, as in the United Kingdom, health is spread over many directorates, which do not liaise well on health issues.

I'm a strong believer in the concept of "health audit" in public policy — that is, the government looking at the health implications of all its policies. This could be based on the World Health Organisation's *Health for All by the Year 2000*[3] targets, many of which are founded on equity.

11

Local health care

The basic information on the health of local communities is poorly collected and presented and there is little interagency collaboration, especially between the health service and local authorities. It is crucial that public health doctors should be able to speak freely in the interests of the community they are employed to serve.

Although I agree in principle with the concept of local representative control, I'm not happy with the concept of local authorities controlling health care. My concern is that they could syphon off money to non-health areas as it is unlikely to be earmarked. It would be better to have a representative "commissioning authority" elected locally on a health ticket to run health.

In principle the health model is no different to education, housing, social services, etc — that is, each has its experts or professionals, but ultimately a democratically elected body takes the strategic decisions.

Assessment of need

In the long term assessment of health needs will be a productive and respected task, just as randomised controlled trials are now accepted as the way to assess effectiveness. There should be a greater emphasis on need in the allocation of funds to regions. Similarly, there are great variations between regions in allocation to districts (in Mersey, for instance, unemployment is used as an indicator of need: this type of approach should be the universal practice).

Purchaser-provider concept

Now that general practitioners have been given the option to control their budgets each fundholding general practitioner has to become his or her own epidemiologist. I'm finding it increasingly difficult to do any real planning on the ground. I can assess needs on a district basis but I cannot really assure appropriate provision any more. The many new influences on general practitioner referral patterns because of the market make sensible planning completely impossible.

I would combine family health services authorities and district health authorities for rational purchasing. I'm worried about the formation of large district health authority consortia for purchasing purposes — in Mersey the 10 district health authorities have formed just two purchasing consortia. In theory these consortia have more purchasing power, but business logic is being applied with little regard to the different needs of the different district health authority populations.

If services are to be planned rationally district health authorities should have a coordinating role over hospital managers; they should be ensuring a comprehensive and effective health service locally with minimum standards based on needs assessment. Hospitals can be managed by operational boards, but there does need to be some coordinating control to avoid duplication of facilities and services (or absence of services).

1 Public Health Alliance. *Beyond Acheson — an agenda for the new public health.* Birmingham: PHA, 1988.
2 Secretary of State for Health. *The health of the nation.* London: HMSO, 1991. (Cm 1523.)
3 World Health Organisation. *Targets for health for all* Copenhagen: WHO, 1985.

Health promotion: planning in Wales

JOHN CATFORD, *executive director, Health Promotion Authority for Wales*

Health promotion

I believe that health promotion is an important part of medical practice. There should be earmarked funds for health promotion because of the very heavy pressure to respond to demands for treatment. At the policy level within the NHS decisions should be taken centrally on the balance of investments that should be made in different policy areas after proper research and consultation. Operational management for health promotion activities should then be delegated as far down as possible and away from the "hands on" influence of politicians and civil servants. In this way there will be a common direction and purpose together with optimum delivery.

Within the NHS operational planning, management, and evaluation in health promotion should take place at primary care, district, and regional levels according to opportunities to influence individuals, organisations, policies, and structures, etc. Partnership is essential, and this can be encouraged through a shared strategic framework.

Regional units

I believe that there should be regional health promotion units. These would be operational units covering populations of 3-5 million and would not only work in the health sector but also in education, local authorities, media, commerce, and industry. This could be associated with regional government in England. Wales and Scotland are already enjoying limited autonomy; English regions should do likewise. With the likely changes in Europe I think that greater autonomy of the United Kingdom regions is essential.

National policy

There should, however, be a joint United Kingdom health policy approach linking with European initiatives. At present the British nations do not always speak with one voice in terms of health policy. I suggest that there could be a health policy group based at the centre but *not* involved operationally, also not dominated by civil servants. I think that *The Health of the Nation*[1] was produced in England because the Department of Health felt left behind by Wales and others. I think that this development could become very civil servant based, with little medical and public health input. To date there has been minimal opportunity for involvement of the health service. A shared policy, jointly "owned" is essential for success.

In the United States there has been a better approach to health strategy planning that uses massive consultation with the health system and consumers. We must keep *The Health of the Nation's* momentum going, but the document can do little on its own and must be followed up. Is there a Department of Health monitoring group? In fact *The Health of the Nation* is a list of aspirations; it is not a real health strategy. Indeed, is the document supported widely within the civil service? Is it a Cabinet or a Department of Health initiative? It must be supported across departments.

Wales

In Wales, health promotion policy is based on consultation and market research. The strategy "Health for All in Wales" took three years to develop by the Health Promotion Authority for Wales (HPAW). Currently work is underway to turn the objectives and targets into tangible plans for action, organisation by organisation, sector by sector. A computerised database has been set up of about 600 organisations whose activities and plans are now being tracked. I believe that effective health promotion needs much more than advertising campaigns; proper market techniques should be used with careful targeting of specific populations which are not too large and have a common identity, language, etc (market segments).

I work as executive director (chief executive) of a special health authority responsible for a range of public health programmes across Wales. In all, 20-25% of the work of the Health Promotion Authority for Wales is with the NHS. A major objective is to encourage other sectors that they have a health promoting responsibility — for example, in the workplace, where a healthier workforce will be a more contented one as well as more productive.

15

I am also professor of health promotion at the University of Wales College of Medicine, with an active multidisciplinary postgraduate training programme (Masters degrees, etc), and a member of the Welsh Health Planning Forum, which has produced a systematic framework for planning in the NHS in Wales. Health authorities have been asked to develop local strategies for health and the setting of health objectives and targets have been encouraged. These have not been prescriptive but I hope that district health authorities will want to contribute to the all Wales health promotion targets proposed by the Health Promotion Authority for Wales. It is important that district health authorities have a real sense of ownership of their own targets. I would really like to see them coming up with their own targets so that the overall Welsh targets can be recalculated.

Purchaser-provider concept

I am concerned that under the purchaser-provider arrangements the formation of a number of purchasing organisations or groups responsible for the same populations — that is, district health authorities, family health services authorities, general practitioner fundholders — could be a real problem. Will fundholders be sensitive to the targets of *The Health of the Nation* in general as opposed to the needs of their own patients as they see them? I think that there has been muddled thinking on this. General practitioners have responsibility for their own individual patients but district health authorities have responsibility for the whole population. Another NHS reorganisation is inevitable after the election.

There should be more work done on health promotion incentives for general practitioners. Should general practitioners be paid partly on results — that is, health outcomes. For instance, should they be rewarded for detecting positive cervical smears, therefore encouraging them to reach high risk groups, or should they be paid for health gain — for instance, measurable reductions in the number of smokers in the practice. However, is general practitioner intervention on a one to one basis actually the correct and most cost effective approach for health promotion? Often the intervention is too little too late — for example, preventing teenage smoking is preferable to helping middle aged smokers to give up.

There should be more cost benefit studies in health promotion so that the health service can buy what is valuable. There has not been an adequate level of resources for research into health promotion and decisions on this are often made in the dark. I'm very dubious about the efficacy of some interventions decided centrally, such as advertising campaigns.

Assessment of need

If money follows the patient can funding be allocated strictly according to need alone, and how will demand be taken into account? At present in this country there is a tendency to fund demand rather than need. With increased patient power the NHS will inevitably become more demand led. This will have an important impact on the ability to achieve the objectives and targets of *The Health of the Nation*. Hence there is a need to have a strong intersectoral programme of health promotion which is safeguarded from demand influences.

1 Secretary of State for Health. *The health of the nation*. London: HMSO, 1991. (Cm 1523.)

Funding for needs

EILEEN WAIN, *chairman, BMA's Committee for Public Health Medicine and Community Health*

Assessment of need

We must start longer term review of need now. We may need to start superficially and be pragmatic because not enough is yet known about effectiveness of treatment and outcomes. We therefore have to use the best present knowledge and start a review which will be part of a continuing cycle of assessment of need.

Task groups

One method which can be used is the setting up of health needs assessment task groups to look at particular conditions — for example, diabetes. The core group should include general practitioners (including fundholders), one or more consultants, and a diabetic liaison nurse, together with a representative from the community health services and the family health services authority. It should be responsible to the Director of Public Health, and I do not believe it appropriate to involve managers at this stage.

One of the aims of the task group should be to arrive at agreed protocols of care so that, for instance, there will be pressure on all local purchasers of care to pay for the whole range of care, including regular eye check ups and chiropody services.

Information on outcome

Consideration needs to be given to making better use of general practice annual reports so that cohorts of patients can be followed up. There is a need to know more about long term outcomes after discharge from hospital, for instance, particularly with the gradual decrease in lengths of stay. Equally, we should be collecting information on morbidity rather than depending on mortality data.

Planning

Planning at district health authority level will very much depend on how much financial and purchasing power is retained at that level. The average general practitioner fundholder will not have significant purchasing clout unless the rules of the game are changed, but I believe that many fundholders will find themselves even more exposed as the numbers increase. The setting up of consortia of fundholders will help, but the cost of administering these will be high; I am therefore optimistic that the district will continue to have a significant purchasing role for the time being.

Purchaser-provider concept

My district had already devolved much management authority to its provider units before the reforms were implemented. The executive directors work as a team, but also accept responsibility within two subgroups: one takes a strategic view and is concerned with purchasing, planning, and consumer affairs, and public health medicine, while the other manages the directly managed units at arm's length and involves the chief executive and finance director. Directly managed units locally have not been given their own independent boards. District general managers have a legal requirement to run the directly managed units, but ours is a purchaser at heart; many of them, however, are still in the provider mould. I accept that accountability for directly managed units could be transferred to the regional health authority if district health authorities were to disappear. This would be better than their being taken over by other self governing trusts to make big monopolies; but this option ignores the fact that all units are likely to become trusts before district health authorities disappear.

It is too early to assess what is happening as a result of the implementation of the purchaser-provider system. Self governing trusts seem to *think* that they are masters and many seem out to strip assets and take over manpower and facilities. In the face of this district health authorities have to be strong and must decide what *they* want to buy. If they do not impose their will as purchasers self governing trusts would be able to concentrate on profitable services which bear little relation to the health needs of the local population.

The contracts which maintain the purchaser-provider system are a bureaucratic nightmare owing to lack of adequate financial net-

19

work and support systems or appropriate information. Would it be more simple to just have a billing system? There would still need to be service agreements and quality standards, but billing for work done rather than contracting prospectively for it might have been much more straightforward.

I support the concept of purchasing as long as it is done on the basis of proper assessment of need and with the money following the patient. I believe that the district health authority or other purchasing authority must have the power to insist that the self governing trust provides a particular service — for instance, there might be a need for designated services for elderly people.

Accountability

Many have expressed concern that the non-executive directors of health authorities are chosen behind closed doors; there is a perception that "political" leanings are to the forefront. One way of dealing with these concerns would be to ensure that part of the selection process should assess candidates' attitudes, knowledge, and commitment. There is a need for known criteria, open assessment, and an independent appointment panel.

I support community health councils in principle, but methods of selection such as those for non-executive directors should be reviewed. It is important that community health councils should be seen to have strong, effective leadership with truly representative members, otherwise there is a real danger that their role will disappear.

Community care

Involvement

Caring for People[1] just will not work if there is not enough funding. We work extremely closely with social services and in my district there are 10 service planning teams; however, differing attitudes to involvement of members, as exists in many parts of the country, does not always make for ease of working.

The service planning teams try to encourage consumer involvement, for instance from the Council for Voluntary Organisations or Age Concern or informal local interest groups. But if individuals from these organisations are to participate effectively in the decision making process they must have training. How is this to be funded?

Residential homes

I am doubtful whether the social security money currently going to residential homes will actually come in to local authorities in 1993. Increasing patient dependency is common in residential homes. Do we need to label residential homes as district health authority or social services (that is, nursing or residential)? Why not consider having joint homes, as has happened in some places, with the district health authority providing the necessary health care support that is missing. This is a good idea in theory, but many districts would be likely to need additional funding for pump-priming such an initiative.

Joint approach

I'm not keen on the model of unitary local authorities commissioning health care. The pre-1948 model of health care can hardly be considered a great success. I can see some benefit, however, in bringing community care (that is, social services) under district health authority control. At present, in order to receive appropriate care, patients have to go through both the NHS and the local authority hoops, yet the present funding and organisational arrangements still create difficulties. A joint approach could at least cut down some of the bureaucracy. On the other hand, if sufficient funding were to be made available for community care plans would such difficulties cease?

Integration of primary and secondary care

Some of the self governing trusts are keen on integration to the extent that they want to increase their outreach services — for example, to appoint their own health visitors to arrange follow up after discharge. This must be of great concern as there is the risk of their being involved in only the interesting bits of work in the community, and therefore this sort of extension of self governing trusts should not be acceptable. We should, however, strengthen primary care and agree discharge protocols to ensure a good level of continuing care when required.

If the number of beds used in the service decreases as expected, the number of district general hospitals decreases, and doctor productivity increases by reducing bed stay, then for consultants to "consult" outside their base hospitals might be something of a relief. This may result in a need to increase the numbers of consultants, as in a socially deprived district, for instance, patients are far more likely to go to a local hospital than up to some big centre in the city. However, this would be one way of ensuring equity of access to those most in need.

1 Secretaries of State for Health, Social Security, Wales, and Scotland. *Caring for people, community care in the next decade and beyond*. London: HMSO, 1989. (Cmnd 849.)

Need for more expenditure on health and safety

JOE KEARNS, *former chairman, BMA's Occupational Health Committee, and chairman, European Communities Committee*

Shortcomings of the NHS

The NHS has never been comprehensive and readily available, and never could have been from its outset. This is "nirvana." Experience has shown that the aim should have been at a minimum standard of health for the nation, measured in terms of suffering and disability. There should be explicit priorities that are understood by the population, decided by politicians, and provided by doctors.

Management

In the past the profession has largely abdicated its responsibilities with regard to management and has acted as though clinical freedom as an ideal should be a right, irrespective of cost. There is now a need for well trained managers who can take on the government of the day on its own terms, demanding much better management information systems — you can't manage what you can't measure. Managers with a basic medical qualification should be involved with planning and strategic decision making, particularly on core issues, to avoid duplication of effort and facilities within the service. There must be better liaison between the NHS and commercial management schools to develop the relationships between managers and technical experts achieved elsewhere, which enable both to contribute more effectively; there could be national vocational qualifications or sandwich courses. The NHS is not an organisation unique in all respects, as it claims to be, but an enterprise engaged in a particular activity.

Other activities

The NHS should stick to dealing with ill health and there should be a separate body to deal with health promotion, prevention, and long term client care.

Doctors' performance

More work must be done by the profession on performance of doctors. Clinical performance is just not assessed at present. Doctors must take the responsibility for colleagues who perform poorly.

Funding

Adequate funding for health care is distorted because patients do not know the cost of their treatment. There must be ways of making these costs constantly evident. One means of doing so would be to require a reimbursement system (such as that in France) so that the patient actually knows the cost of treatment as it is delivered, though much of it is reimbursed.

Research and development

There should be more research into outcomes and effectiveness of treatment and more money generally put into medical research within the NHS. This research should be not only on clinical areas but on the cost benefit of health promotion and the cost effectiveness of treatments generally. A proper programme of research and development is needed not only to control and coordinate local innovation but encourage it too. Centres of excellence in a particular field should undertake development work and, perhaps, licence treatments as drugs are currently licensed. Research and development money would need to be top sliced to subsidise innovative work and therefore promote it — that is, to encourage purchasers to use innovative treatments.

Occupational health

The lifting of crown immunity from the NHS demands much greater expenditure on health and safety to meet standards already well established in industry as a legal requirement. Health and safety funding and activity should be included in managers' performance review. A culture of personal accountability for health and safety for oneself and one's colleagues and subordinates should also be encouraged (for example, in relation to use of sharps). There should be a credible career structure to enable occupational health training within the NHS, which currently has no postgraduate training units. This would benefit both the service and industry as medical and paramedical staff would gain a greatly enhanced understanding of rehabilitation, while the many small enterprises and individuals served by NHS occupational departments would for the first time be cared for during the working hours in which their earnings and wellbeing are determined.

PATIENTS, PRIMARY CARE, AND THE COMMUNITY

Patients' rights and participation in health care policy

LINDA LAMONT, *director, Patients Association*

Patients' rights

I believe that all patients should have "the right to health care appropriate to their needs, whether for acute primary or community care and regardless of their ability to pay" (Patients Association charter). Health is a basic right or need equivalent to food and housing. I'm not sure that the government accepts this philosophy.

The Patients Association argues that all patients should have the choice of general practitioner, a second opinion, treatment, hospital, sex of the doctor, and residential care or domiciliary services, and that there should be realistic support for the carers who make it possible for patients to stay at home. In relation to quality, the good of the patient must always be considered as a priority against costs.

The views of patients and their representatives should play an integral part in setting and monitoring standards of health care. When information centres are set up for patients there should be a facility for collecting data on their comments and complaints; this consumer comment could be used to improve services and could be fed into work on effectiveness and outcome of treatment.

An example of a right patients currently enjoy under the general practitioner contract is a health check for patients who have not seen a doctor for three years. This is seen as a useful "MOT" by many patients but apparently as a tiresome exercise of unproved value by many general practitioners. Such a conflict of views seems incongruous in the light of the current discussions about how to improve preventive health measures. There is room for discussion about what tests should be included, but the principle of having the check up should remain.

Complaints procedures

I'm not happy with complaints procedures generally, but particularly in the private sector. This deficiency will become increasingly relevant as more patients are referred to the private sector from the NHS under the new purchaser-provider arrangements. For similar reasons I'm concerned that members of community health councils can visit private hospitals and nursing homes only if they are invited, and even if invited the reports they can produce are limited in scope.

A key proposal from the Patients Association concerning the patient's charter is the setting up of a health consumer standards board. The responsibility of the board would be to consult with patients in order to set and monitor the standards of health care which people are entitled to expect. An independent inspectorate with a lay element should report on local performance in conjunction with users, representative bodies like community health councils, and self help groups. I support the work of the Audit Commission, which should continue to perform studies in particular areas, but I see the Health Consumer Standards Board as a quite distinct organisation which would work in conjunction with management and professional bodies.

Accountability

In general terms there should be accountability through a clearly defined chain of command so that there is always a specified person or department responsible for the individual patient's care. This will be particularly complex when community care plans are implemented. More specifically, in relation to health authorities, I have a real concern about the selection of non-executive directors who are in no way representative of local communities, very few of whom, incidentally, are women.

Non-executive directors should actually live in the local community. I accept that the old health authorities were not ideal. Both selection and election have their merits and problems. We need better criteria for either method and accredited training for lay members of health authorities, as well as other lay people working in health fields (for example, on community health councils). During the selection process evidence should be shown of knowledge about how the NHS works or, at least, the ability to acquire new knowledge quickly. The whole process should be much more open to scrutiny and non-executive director posts should be advertised. I think that five lay non-executive directors is too small a number, if only because so much work has to be shared out.

While it is important that consumers' representatives should play a major part in the decisions related to the provision of health care, the relationship between representatives and the district health authority should not be too cosy. I'm a strong supporter of community health councils, but they need more teeth (for example, rights of access) and more resources. I recognise that the councils are very patchy and suggest that selection of members should take more account of voluntary groups working in the community.

Waiting lists: keeping patients informed

MARIANNE RIGGE, *director, College of Health*

Assessment of need

Consumer audit

Information on need is at present primarily epidemiological, and I believe that this does not necessarily reflect real patient need. The College of Health believes strongly in "consumer audit" to complement other more familiar means of assessment such as clinical audit, organisational audit, and value for money audit. I accept that consumer audit is not easy and not cheap, but the aim is to look at the service provided from the patient's point of view and to give full emphasis to emotional as well as physical wellbeing and to the quality and clarity of communication.

Lack of communication

I have been involved in a survey assessing the quality of life for patients waiting for orthopaedic procedures and when discharged after the procedure. This and other surveys demonstrate a vast amount of unrecognised unmet need. For instance, the circumstances of the patient may have changed since the last outpatient appointment over a year before. I'm concerned about the lack of communication with waiting patients by hospitals; do they realise that many patients hardly dare go out while waiting in case the call for admission comes?

There is a desperate need for clinical validation or prioritisation on a regular basis. Perhaps a triage nurse or district nurse could do a home assessment or else there should be an outpatient appointment for all those waiting on, say, a six monthly basis. There is also a need for much better communication between general practitioners and consultants; general practitioners could report changes in their patients' condition to consultants, taking into account factors such as home circumstances, which could be assessed by health visitors. The College of Health is now operating its waiting list telephone helpline. In terms of waiting times for operations orthopaedics is the main problem; then general surgery; ophthalmology; and ear, nose, and throat surgery. I'm also concerned about access to specialist outpatient departments and particularly the uneven nature of specialist cover around the country's district health authorities; apparently there are some 39 district health authorities with no cardiologist and a further significant number, for instance, with no specialist rheumatology service.

Prioritisation

There is a need for informed debate both on the need for prioritisation and how it is to be undertaken. The medical profession could do a lot more by involving lay people in discussions on types of treatment priorities — the involvement of lay people in the King's Fund forum consensus statements was a good start. As well as looking at comparative risks and alternative forms of treatment there should be proper analysis of patients' views through the sort of surveys that the College of Health has been doing.

Accountability

District health authorities should be much more accountable to local populations. They should somehow involve the public in planning of provision and assessment of need. I support community health councils and believe that the councils' representatives should have access to all parts of health authority meetings. I'm concerned about the development of self governing trusts not least because of the lack of any real consultation with anybody; one advantage of trusts which is developing, however, is that they are putting out more information about their clinics and facilities.

I am generally happy with the concept of the general practitioner as a proxy for the consumer, but general practitioners should nevertheless be seen to be asking the patients more about what they want from the practice. General practitioners are now involved in medical audit but I believe that they should also be doing more consumer audit.

In relation to the hospital service, doctors should be prepared to deal more explicitly with substandard consultants. Doctors know who these consultants are, but if they continue to allow a system where these doctors can still practise it reflects badly and damages professional credibility generally. In hospitals there should also be increased management accountability; often hospitals have nameless information officers and it can be very difficult for patients to find out "where the buck stops."

Community care

I think it scandalous that so little has been done on care in the community and that there is no sign of proper funding for the implementation of *Caring for People*.[1] There is a need for collaboration among all the parties concerned and each area should have a "community care coordinator," who knows what is going on, who can communicate with the various agencies concerned, and whom patients can call for advice.

1 Secretaries of State for Health, Social Security, Wales, and Scotland. *Caring for people, community care in the next decade and beyond*. London: HMSO, 1989. (Cmnd 849.)

The need for a flexible approach

JULIAN TUDOR HART, *general practitioner, West Glamorgan, and Department of General Practice, St Mary's Hospital*

The new GP contract

My paper entitled "Twenty five years of case finding and audit in a socially deprived community"[1] is a reasonable model for planning a shift of care towards the deprived population. If I had been asked to write a new general practitioner contract 25 years ago I admit that I would probably have produced something like the present contract, but my ideas since then have changed considerably with the experience of applying them in practice. I am concerned about the setting of outcome objectives. I believe that the means of attaining objectives should not be specified because there will always be a diversity of solutions.

Incentives

Doctors should have clinical incentives to do satisfying work; if this is not the case then something has to be done about medical training. Restoring the dignity and self confidence of doctors would achieve much more than economic incentives.

The first general practitioner charter[2] was good in that the Department of Health stopped putting money directly into general practitioners' pockets and began to put it into the practice — for example, for facilities and ancillary staff. In the second charter (the new general practitioner contract)[3] the earlier approach should have been continued with more funding coming into practices — for instance, for information technology.

Patient care

Before the new contract was imposed I believe that there had been a developing cooperative relationship between general prac-

35

titioners and patients. Patients seemed to be taking more responsibility for their own illnesses and doctors were accepting their responsibility to keep patients better informed. A principal objective for the BMA should be to protect this beneficial development — that is, to continue to allow patients and general practitioners to set their own objectives by collaborating together. Family health services authorities should be encouraged to allow a flexible approach to the contract (as long as they are sure that there is no outright fraud going on). I believe that about 40–50% of practices are really serious about trying to improve patient care and that the "scoundrels" amount to less than 5%, the rest being largely apathetic. The real innovators in relation to patient care need neither sticks nor carrots, but support for their work.

Area administratiion

The BMA should also consider the role of family health services authorities seriously. Area administration will be important; the correct unit size for administration and epidemiological assessment is around 50 000 to 100 000, whereas the correct unit size for dealing with patients is perhaps 10 000 for a group and 1700 for one general practitioner. Fundholding practices will be too small for sensible, cost effective administration.

The educational approach

I strongly believe that there are better ways of handling general practitioners than giving them cash limited budgets or using other types of incentives. The educational approach does work; for instance, prescribing analysis and cost (PACT) has reduced per capita prescribing costs since its introduction in 1988. For apparently ideological reasons the Department of Health does not appear to be interested in these types of data and wants only to use financial incentives to get things done.

Accountability

I believe that local government should be responsible for health in the widest sense. I accept that the government has stripped dignity and authority from local government, yet local authorities are crucial for local democracy. I have been a local councillor and was impressed with the high priority given to health issues but also struck by the complete lack of knowledge and understanding of those same issues.

One of the worst features of the self governing trusts and of the new district health authorities is their lack of accountability to the local community. District health authorities should have elected members to ensure local accountability. In relation to general practitioner accountability, organised patient participation should be taken more seriously; for instance, annual reports should be written with an audience of patients in mind and should cover achievements, obstacles, and targets.

In relation to health promotion, clinics have so far been assumed to be detection clinics rather than follow up clinics. The problem is that not much thought has been given to what has to be done after detection.

Conclusion

General practice must be allowed to develop flexibly, but I believe that it is easier to "purchase" hospital care because it is much more process orientated. General practitioners have a wide ranging role, and meddling with prescription and financial incentives may not be beneficial to patients in the long run.

1 Tudor Hart J, Thomas C, Gibbons B, Edwards C, Hart M, Jones J, et al. Twenty five years of case funding and audit in a socially deprived community. BMJ 1991; 302: 1509–13.
2 BMA. Charter for the family doctor service, London: BMA, 1965.
3 Department of Health. A new contract for general practice. London: HMSO, 1991.

Competition among providers

MICHAEL GOLDSMITH, *former general practitioner trainer, director, Medisure, and research fellow, Centre for Policy Studies*

General practitioner as purchasers

In my original proposals for health service reform[1-3] family practitioner committees — now family health services authorities — were to be the prime purchasers. A health maintenance organisation needs a minimum of about 100 000 subscribers or population for cost effective, non-wasteful resourcing. The current fundholder size, therefore, is too small, whereas the family health services authority has adequate buying power and spread of population. The concept of general practitioner cooperatives is interesting, but the combined list size would still be too small for sensible budgeting.

The market model should be of competing *providers* rather than competing purchasers — that is, fundholding practices, groups of practices, and health authorities. A further difficulty with fundholding is where there are monopoly providers. In these cases the provider contracts would have to be extremely tight on quality and standards. It would still be possible, however, if a bad service is provided for the secretary of state to change the board or management; an alternative would be the building of a competing private hospital.

Nevertheless, I believe that fundholders will increase in number, but, when they reach a critical mass in a family health services authority area, they could form a fundholding negotiating committee within the authority to organise their purchasing. In due course it would be sensible for the family health services authority to purchase on behalf of all practices, but there would have to be very strong general practitioner input into the negotiations as the authority would, in effect, be providing a service for general practitioners as a professional purchasing organisation.

I accept that family health services authorities could become wings of district health authorities, in which case the district health authority would become the purchasers and the regional health authority would allocate funds.

Quality assurance

If the district health authorities or family health services authorities became purchasers they would still need to keep their policing role of both the public and private sectors. However, I believe that there should be an inspectorate of health care, as there is an inspectorate of prisons. In the absence of this, family health services authorities — if purchasers on behalf of general practitioners — should certainly inspect providers with whom they have contracts to ensure they have adequate quality assurance and standards.

I believe that there should also be inspection of general practitioners. Otherwise how do members of the public decide on their general practitioner? Each family health services authority should have a small inspecting team of, say, three people, including a manager, a doctor, and a lay person (or a panel of such people from whom inspecting teams would be chosen). The team would need to spend a minimum of about two hours each year in each practice, and also a sample of perhaps 10% of the patients in each practice would get a quality assurance questionnaire. I'm not too happy with the term "accreditation" but, in due course, why shouldn't practices get gold, silver, and bronze awards?

Polyclinics

I'm keen on the concept of "one stop shopping," where a whole range of services including doctors, nurses, dentists, chiropodists, pharmacists, etc, is available in one centre. Community nursing services should be devolved from district health authorities and either financed by the practice directly or by the family health services authority. An even more radical idea would be for community trusts to employ all primary care team staff, including general practitioners, to provide a broad range of services in the community.

Planning and assessment of need

Much tighter definition is required. Public health doctors should do the epidemiological work in relation to handing down cash to practices, but general practitioners must be involved in the exercise — that is, practices should contribute to the planning round. Clearly, proper information technology systems would become essential to ensure the appropriate data collection, along with a common coding system such as the Reed classification. Regional health authorities should really become regional planning authorities, and if too large for this some regions may need to be divided up further — for example, into areas.

Accountability

Centrally, I'm not keen on the arm's length, corporation approach, although I accept some devolution of executive power to the NHS Management Executive. Locally, I like the idea of a health watchdog body (almost a quality circle concept) associated with each provider unit. There is more difficulty with the concept of involving consumers in local planning. I'm not happy with the community health council system or with reintroducing party politics on to district health authority boards. We particularly need informed opinion to do the job; perhaps there could be a "health bench," whose members would have teeth and would report to the family health services authority or district health authority board and would be chosen along similar lines to justices of the peace — that is, through a regional commission and inclusion of interviews on attitudes, politics, etc.

Funding

It is imperative that the service is principally funded from the centre to ensure health care for all, including the disadvantaged. I'm against a hypothecated health tax. It would start a precedent and make fiscal planning extremely difficult. People could vote for huge increases, which would put a serious problem on to other areas of public spending; the system could also be extremely inflexible.

I believe that there are arguments for increased funding. These could be built round better assessment of needs and round the government's current interest in a people's charter. Incidentally, I believe that money for health and social services from employers might be better raised as corporation tax rather than National Insurance as corporation tax does not have to be paid when a company is not in profit.

There should be a system of copayments to add extra funding. I support prescription and dental charges but believe that eye test charges were a big mistake in view of the role of eye examination in prevention. I would provide the core health service free but the "bits and pieces" might be charged for and could certainly be insured for at various levels — ranging from third party to full cover. I would include hotel charges for luxurious facilities in hospitals, cosmetic surgery, possibly chiropody, in vitro fertilisation, treatments for infertility, etc. I would also charge £2-5 for patients wishing to make a routine general practitioner visit and copayments for home visits and possibly even outpatient visits (as long as there was no significant wait, in which case the money would be returned).

I accept the concept of raising extra money through local taxation as long as this is seen as putting icing on the cake rather than paying for a new cake. Core funding should come from the centre, but more could be raised through the poll tax, particularly for care in the community. I accept that the Griffiths model for community care[4] is the best on offer, but I'm greatly concerned about funding, and particularly the lack of ringfencing.

I find the idea of a compulsory private health insurance quite interesting but I am extremely concerned about the recent change to give tax relief on health insurance to elderly people. I think that tax relief is very inefficient and leads to increased costs in the long run.

1 Goldsmith M, Willetts D. *Managed health care: a new system for a better health service.* London: Centre for Policy Studies, 1988.
2 Willetts D, Goldsmith M. *A mixed economy for health care: more spending, same taxes.* London: Centre for Policy Studies, 1988.
3 Goldsmith M, Pirie M. *Managing better health.* London: Adam Smith Institute, 1988
4 Griffiths R. *Community care: agenda for action.* London: HMSO, 1988

The role of community health councils

TOBY HARRIS, *director, Association of Community Health Councils of England and Wales*

Accountability

Central accountability

I am worried by the increasing trend to deny central accountability (for example, the speech made by Baroness Cumberlege to the Institute of Health and Safety in Medicine, in which she welcomed the fact that parliamentary officials were rejecting questions to ministers on local health service matters, saying that they should be dealt with by local management). This cannot be a good thing in terms of accountability. It will probably mean that ministers will avoid having to answer difficult questions but that they will still meddle in local affairs when it suits them. In reality, the centre has as much control over the health service as it has ever had and should accept the accountability that goes with it.

Local accountability

I'm aware that there were two principal alternative models for local accountability being promoted: firstly, direct elections to health authorities (that is, yet another body to vote for) and, secondly, the Institute for Public Policy Research (IPPR) model of health services being run by local authorities. It is important to recognise that you cannot have real local autonomy without local accountability. If we are going to go down this road some local taxation base for health authorities would have to be considered in the longer term (over the next 5-10 years).

Purchaser-provider concept

I have serious doubts about certain aspects of the purchaser-provider split as proposed in the NHS and Community Care Act. I recognise, however, that one positive byproduct has been the requirement for purchasers to have to specify what has to be delivered. As a result, it should be possible to build in quality standards and value for money.

The market will, however, need to be carefully regulated. In theory, regional health authorities could do this, but perhaps regulators should be even more distant from the "coal face." It would be possible to augment the Audit Commission or introduce a "Quality Commission," but measures would have to be taken to avoid these becoming large bureaucracies. If regulation is to be carried out at regional level one possibility would be some form of joint regional health and social services inspectorate. This would be more independent than the current "arm's length" social services inspectorate run by the social services and would introduce a new health inspectorate. I believe that this or any other regulatory body must have input from lay people and patients.

Community health councils

Community health councils do not need to merge, even if district health authorities merge; it is important to maintain links with grass roots local opinion. The councils will have a particular role to inform purchasers of consumer opinion — hopefully formal channels will be set up, perhaps through community health council representatives as non-voting but participating observers at purchaser boards. The councils should also feed in strongly to any system of regulation which is set up (see above). If patient information points are set up in hospitals (as suggested in the patient's charter) then community health councils should be involved, both to keep in touch with patients' views and to inform them.

Funding

While *The Health of the Nation* document[1] is in some respects disappointing, I strongly support the idea of providing a framework of health targets. We will need to build up a national pattern, through proper needs assessment locally, to inform the process. If specific parameters and targets can be set this would help to stop health being seen as a bottomless pit in relation to funding.

There also needs to be an explicit public demand on priorities and choice for funding. This has to be wider than the one to one doctor-patient relationship. This is all part of the partnership and empowerment concept — that is, there will be a better outcome if the patient feels part of the decision making process. More resources are clearly needed for health care, and greater patient involvement will increase the pressure on governments for better funding.

1 Secretary of State for Health. *The health of the nation*. London: HMSO, 1991. (Cm 1523.)

Funding and deprived areas

ROS LEVENSON, *director, Greater London Association of Community Health Councils*

Accountability

I have no faith that non-executive directors of health authorities are at all accountable to the local population, nor could one expect them to be as it is not laid down in the NHS and Community Care Act. Individual directors may or may not have local networks, but I'm not aware of any structural links being established by directors to secure views of local patients in London.

I believe that health authorities should have a large elected component with the chairman being elected by the authority. I would be happy to see local authorities running health. If members of local authorities can deal with education and social services they can deal with health — when dealing with education councillors are not asked to teach but to sort out the policy issues. I accept that local authorities are very party political but believe that explicit politics merely open up what might otherwise be hidden.

Purchaser-provider concept

There is a need for some purchaser-provider split, and there is an increasing consensus on this. A plethora of purchasers, however, will not allow a strategic approach to the assessed needs of the population.

I favour the combination of family health services authorities and district health authorities so long as primary care can be adequately provided. Purchasing *through* the health authority is the sensible public health approach. The alternative of general practitioner fundholders purchasing direct (that is, the each competes with the other approach) may be less beneficial for patients with the greater incentive being to "work the system." This would exacerbate class inequalities in health.

The current fundholding scheme may work only when the fundholders are in a minority. Once the numbers get larger the advantages being extracted for patients will reduce. Fundholding may work best where a large number of patients on the list are privately insured and can be persuaded not to use the NHS, but that is only from the fundholder's point of view. From the patient's point of view it would undermine the fundamental concept of a national health service.

Self governing trusts

Firstly, I am extremely concerned by the process through which trusts were established. There was little meaningful consultation, an unwillingness to listen, and a paucity of useful financial information provided. Secondly, I believe that if more autonomy is given to providers in London then they are almost bound to plan services which may not necessarily be in the best interests of Londoners — that is, they do not necessarily see Londoners as customers, so a situation could arise where there are many London beds but not for Londoners themselves.

If purchasers call the shots then the purchaser-provider split can be beneficial, but if providers have a monopoly (specialist or geographical) there is a serious problem and the whole market concept fails. Also, I do not accept the appropriateness of market concepts to health care provision.

Community care

I have serious doubts as to whether anybody will stick to the 1993 timetable for the implementation of *Caring for People*[1]; Griffiths's proposals are fine, but only if properly funded. In addition to the problems of delivery there will need to be a great deal of training in preparation, but few resources are available for this. I fully support the need to ringfence funds for care in the community; there should also be more central guidance on standards for community care. There will continue to be a need for some institutional care, particularly respite care, both for elderly people and for those with learning difficulties.

I regard the model of the work being done for those with HIV

46

infection in the community as an interesting analogy. There has been a mix of community support, respite, and residential care, together with a large voluntary sector, within the framework of largely public funding. This has worked well in many places but has been enormously expensive for the relatively small numbers of patients. This shows what can be done when appropriate priority is given.

Funding

Allocation of funds

Allocation of funds within London is a real problem, particularly in relation to the homeless, whose needs are not given due account in capitation funding, and to transients. There needs to be more allowance for local deprivation: sometimes tiny communities may be severely deprived but are missed in the overall scheme of things — that is, there needs to be a proper focus to ensure reasonably targeted funding where appropriate. The needs of black and ethnic minority communities must be met, not just endlessly surveyed.

Assessing need is vital and it is particularly necessary to show what impact any extra funding would have on the target.

Raising funds

I believe that if private fund raising was to be a major source of income (through voluntary contributions and lotteries, for instance) health care would be dictated by whim and fashion — the telethon mentality. This tends to support high tech equipment but not the staff to run it and tends to play up patients as victims.

I can see benefits of raising local tax for health, but it is difficult to have financial ownership without political accountability. I'm firmly wedded to a national health service but think that some extra money could be obtained from local authority sources through the joint planning process.

Voluntary sector

The voluntary sector will become a major provider to local authorities, and possibly eventually to health authorities. It is a principal provider for social care and for those with learning or physical disability. What will the accountability of the voluntary agencies be? Will it be through the purchaser? There is a great divide between the larger more powerful voluntary organisations and the smaller ones. I'm concerned that some of the smaller organisations will be squeezed out financially. I'm also worried that as providers voluntary organisations might be less able to have an advocacy and campaigning role.

Community health councils

Even with a fully democratically elected health authority we would still need properly resourced community health councils with access to information and the right to be consulted and listened to. There should be an *independent* establishing authority for community health councils as regional health authorities, which currently have the authority, might well have a conflict of interest in view of their other roles.

I accept some of the criticism of the membership of community health councils, but believe that this criticism comes from people in the health service who feel threatened rather than from the people in the community. The councils rarely divide on political grounds and the regional health authority can balance membership through its nominations. I accept that they do not necessarily "represent" the community but they can facilitate the involvement of community groups through their networks. This enabling and facilitating role is as important as representation.

I believe that there should be lay involvement in medical audit through community health councils.

1 Secretaries of State for Health, Social Security, Wales, and Scotland. *Caring for people, community care in the next decade and beyond*. London: HMSO, 1989. (Cmnd 849.)

SECONDARY CARE AND EDUCATION

Teamwork and collaboration

STEPHEN HUNTER, *consultant in psychological medicine, and former chairman, BMA's Junior Doctors Committee*

Assessment of need

There has been a tendency to make needs assumptions rather than assessments, particularly in psychiatry. Need has been assumed for a certain amount of acute, long stay, day care, and community provision. Nevertheless, strategic plans for the care of the mentally ill in Gwent now accept that the overwhelming majority of psychiatric patients do not need day care, special housing, or social care. These are required by only some 4-5% of the mentally ill; the rest can be treated as outpatients (often in a community setting) or by general practitioners. It is well known, for instance, that the incidence of schizophrenia is dropping; however, chronic conditions like senile dementia do require facilities, and its future prevalence can be quite accurately predicted.

Community care

Planning for the mentally ill and, particularly, the mentally handicapped involves user groups, nurses, managers, and social services, as well as doctors. The approach tends to depend on the relative power strengths of the various players. In mental handicap the local authority tends to plan provision and the consultants do not feel involved. In mental illness the management is dominated by clinicians, so the other players do not feel involved. Both approaches are as bad as each other; there must be proper collaboration.

Wales has a good mental illness strategy, with prioritisation of funds both for capital and revenue. There has been no particular wish, therefore, for the hospitals to become self governing — one of the major attractions of self governing hospitals is the cheap capital which can be borrowed against.

I'm content with the proposals of the second Griffiths report,[1] but I'm concerned about the funding, at least in part because access to support through social security funds is flexible and open ended, particularly with the health authority topping up the funds. I can see the advantages of ringfencing money for community care, but I'm worried that, if it comes, this will actually act as a cash limit. Gearing, in relation to local authority finance, is important because it will cost the poll tax payer more to raise the significant extra finance — since the recent local tax changes the local authority budget raised from local taxation is much smaller, so to raise locally any significant sums for community care will mean a dramatic increase in the local taxes.

Funding and prioritisation

I support the concept of a hypothecated tax for health in order to capitalise on the perceived willingness of the population to pay extra tax if it is for health. National Insurance could be used as the vehicle for this; if money for social services, unemployment, etc, was taken out, at a 9% rate of contribution, this would probably just about pay for the health budget. This would, in itself, encourage open political debate on funding.

The public and the profession have to acknowledge that there must be cash limits. In the past prioritisation has taken place in a covert and clandestine way, mainly by doctors but also by managers. I'm not too happy about the Oregon approach, however; I think it is extremely risky and liable to political and media manipulation. Debates on priorities are probably better focused at a local level.

Effectiveness and audit

The profession has to accept audit, peer review, standard setting, etc. Treatments must be shown to be effective and doctors must be seen to be cost effective. This is a major challenge, but, as in Scotland, consultants should be more prepared to work in teams to enable proper peer review and standard setting. This will mean some sacrifice of individual clinical autonomy that can only benefit both the patient and the profession in the long run.

We will also need better postgraduate education, with opportunities for retraining and recertification and, perhaps, more encouragement of sabbaticals to this end. In the end the 5% or so who refuse to join in (as shown by the confidential enquiry into postoperative deaths (CEEPOD)) may need to be disciplined; this will become a management duty unless the profession is prepared to take on this responsibility more seriously.

Purchaser-provider concept

I believe that the purchaser-provider split is a political rather than an economic concept. I can see benefits in contracts in that they should lead to greater efficiency and better standards. At present, however, the contracts are almost meaningless as they are being set on the basis of inadequate information and inadequate quality standards.

Consultants

We probably need more consultants, particularly if more consultant outpatient work is done in the community. Consultants will continue to have responsibilities but will have diminished power. I believe that the resource management initiative and clinical directorates, however, can lead to both increased influence and job satisfaction — if a consultant is efficient then he or she may be able to expand the service. In relation to consultant contracts, we should at least be considering the possibility of item of service payments, primary care lead payments, and performance related pay (possibly as an alternative to merit awards). A way into this would be to allow contractual and work diversification within the consultant grade. Ultimately those with contracts have to be accountable to peer and management review.

Nurses

As consultants can expand their role into the community, so should the role of nurses and midwives be extended. Nurses are already involved in day patient work, stoma care, giving diabetes advice, and counselling; there is a big debate over intravenous injections, but this could be resolved if giving such injections became part of the nurses' core curriculum. In general practice the nurse could become a filter for the general practitioner, which would both be of real assistance and give professional satisfaction. I accept that there are conflicts, particularly in relation to training; nurses

53

have specifically sought to exclude doctors as trainers, but there is room for both professions to have a role in training each other.

Manpower

There should probably be a full review of the whole staffing structure. Doctors are extremely expensive to train and eventually undertake a vast diversity of tasks. Why is there only one top career grade in primary and secondary care? There are generally too few consultants for genuine service needs but too many for all of them to be managers or clinical directors. If consultants are going to do most of the real hands on work we may need as many as 30 000, but if there is going to be a consultant oligarchy we could need only about 7000.[2]

At the end of the day the patients want quality and to be seen by fully trained doctors. Therefore, more general practitioners are also needed. Patient dissatisfaction is generally with the process of their care rather than the medical treatment; their concern, for instance, is with increased waiting times in hospitals and decreased "time, touch, and compassion" from professionals. I support the concept of organisational audit, but to whom should the resulting information be made available? Should there be Michelin guides to hospitals or to training posts?

Training

There should also be a fundamental review of postgraduate training. Training for general practice is a good model. Accreditation must be properly applied with later recertification if necessary. Training funds in the NHS are poor; in industry generally 4-5% of the budget is ringfenced for training. In this respect East Anglia is one of the best regional health authorities, with 0.8% of the medical budget targeted for training.

1 Griffiths R. *Community care: agenda for action.* London: HMSO, 1988.
2 Scotland A. Consultant oligarchy or worker's cooperative? *Br J Hosp Med* 1990; **44**: 152.

Breaking down the divide

SIR DILLWYN WILLIAMS, *former chairman, Conference of Medical Royal Colleges*

Problems in the NHS

The following key problems face the health service: the management framework within which money is spent; the need for the profession to control its own in relation to the use of resources; and the level at which money is turned into resources. This level should not be too high nor right at the sharp end (that is, fundholders or individual consultant's budgets), so in hospitals budgets should be at hospital or clinical directorate level and in primary care should be for a unit larger than 10 000 patients to avoid wasting a great deal of money on practice management and administration.

It is important to break down the general practice and hospital divide, but the reforms could make matters worse. Contracts could be kept at district health authority level, defining quantity and quality for the whole district — that is, a contract would be needed only for, say, another district health authority taking over a whole ear, nose, and throat service. Contracts for individual treatments or investigations would be needed only when the service was highly complex or extremely expensive.

Clinical directorates

I believe that there should be district wide clinical directorates — including a general practice directorate — with general practitioners sitting on each directorate. This would encourage joint ownership between general practitioners and consultants and less wasteful interhospital rivalry. There is a need for a sensible district based planning system that is not hospital dominated. All directorates, including general practice directorates, should run formal resource

55

management; this would make the general practitioners sit down together with the consultants to decide on the best and most cost effective care.

Contracts for professional services should be made with major specialty groupings, including primary care, as both hospitals and general practitioners are providers. The consultant and general practitioner members of directorates would have to agree the proportion of care to be provided between primary and secondary care. I believe that this would lead to better integration of patient care.

Purchaser-provider concept

I would support the purchaser-provider concept, but only if fundholding and self governing trusts were scrapped to reduce the potential split between general practitioners and consultants.

Purchasing authorities must be able to better determine need if they are to purchase to cover it. In particular, they will need better consumer input than is currently provided by community health councils; these should be scrubbed or amalgamated with the purchasing authorities. The health authority board should include doctors (possibly from other areas), other professionals, and local people, including council members. I believe that if people are elected to local government they should be able to have a say in local health care.

Accountability

If finance is to be handed down to regions on a weighted capitation basis there should be even less need to maintain a huge central bureaucracy. Most of the administration could be devolved to regional health authorities, but strong professional advisory machinery must be kept centrally for ministers, including the chief medical officer and the chief nursing officer.

I would dismantle the NHS Management Executive and concentrate on regions. Targets and health strategy should be set up at regional health authority level. I advocate a similar approach to that used in Wales. The more that can be done at regional health authority level the better as the regional health authority is closer to its own patients and better able to determine their needs. This will mean, however, that the profession will need to provide advice much more effectively to the region. I'm sure that a unit of about 5 million people would be much easier to plan for than the United Kingdom's total population.

Nevertheless, I believe that there should be imposition of certain safety and quality standards from the centre and central negotiation of terms and conditions of service.

Innovation

I recognise that the service increment for teaching and research (SIFTR) money has tended to go to teaching districts. There could be a separate "advancement of clinical practice" grant to encourage innovation and medical development work — that is, it would not just be paid on the basis of efficiency or cost effectiveness. The grant could be allocated by the regional health authority.

Quality standards, costings, and the London problem

CYRIL CHANTLER, *clinical dean, United Medical and Dental Schools of Guy's and St Thomas's Hospitals*

Funding

I'm very concerned about the funding arguments that compare the percentage of the gross domestic product spent on health in the United Kingdom unfavourably with that spent in other countries. Part of the problem is the relatively poor economic performance of the United Kingdom, which is reflected in the fact that the wages and salaries of those working in the service are rather lower than those working in other health services. This is not the whole story, however, and the figure shows the amount spent on health care related to the gross domestic product for various countries, the relationships being shown with the conversions to dollars made by money market rates. Conversions are also made by relating different currencies according to what a unit of currency actually buys in goods and services in that country by using purchasing power parities; the United Kingdom is spot on the purchasing power regression line. I agree that more money is needed, but lack of money is not the only problem.

Assessment of need

I believe that the proposal to strengthen the arguments for improved funding by using assessment of need aggregated over the country would be using "yesterday's language," but I fully accept that much better assessment of need is necessary to ensure sensible allocation of funds, as long as it is done in relation to clinical efficiency and effectiveness.

I believe that the United Kingdom is little different to most other countries, who are all having problems with funding health care and meeting the demand. I'm a passionate believer in the NHS but feel

58

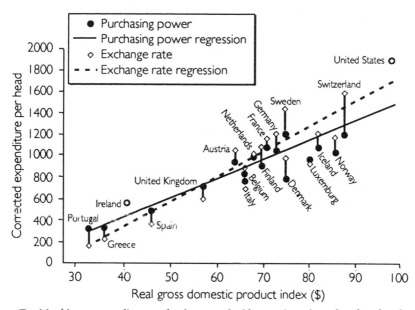

Total health care expenditure per head compared with gross domestic product for selected countries, 1986. Expenditure is expressed in dollars converted by exchange rates and purchasing power parities.

that the service has not been meeting consumer demands. In 1984 Polly Toynbee said, "as charity cases British patients have been willing to put up with long waits, dilapidated hospitals and surgeries, and a lack of consumer choice they would not easily tolerate in most other aspects of their lives. Unless the needs and wishes of the patients are catered for soon, I believe that many of them will start voting with their feet and leave the service that until now they have, in the main, admired and even loved, warts and all."[1]

Quality standards

I'm quite sure that if the NHS is not reformed to provide a better service for consumers more and more patients will move to the insurance or private sector and the concept of a national health service for all will be gone. Quality embraces both consumer satisfaction and medical outcome. In a service with limited cash quantity is also an issue of quality because a high cost service with limited access may deny treatment to someone who would benefit if a cheaper service was provided. One approach is to define acceptable

59

standards of quality and then strive for maximum efficiency to increase quantity.

Resource management

I'm sure that resource management (that is, clinical efficiency) and medical audit (that is, clinical effectiveness) must be linked. I am therefore a strong believer in the resource management initiative and clinical directorates, but the information systems, which must also be developed to improve communication and efficiency within hospitals, must be tailored to the structure and to the needs of clinicians rather than to the needs of accountants.

Purchaser-provider concept

I believe that the introduction of the purchaser-provider concept was necessary and that it is an exercise in decentralisation. I'm extremely concerned that the market could become chaotic and very difficult to control; for instance, wasteful duplication needs to be avoided.

I much prefer the model which gives a regulatory role to the region. I believe that accountability of self governing trusts will be devolved to the region before long, that the region should seek to ensure enough competition to enable choice (even between highly specialist, supraregional type services), and that capital development should be controlled by the region.

I believe in the concept of trusts, not least to allow hospitals freedom from health authority bureaucracy. In relation to terms and conditions of service I accept that they are often, at present, monopoly employers, but this will be less of a problem as the number of trusts increases. Medical salaries are not a real issue as they are only a comparatively small proportion of the salary budget; consultant tenure is more of a problem — I'm not convinced of the need for the continuation of the appeal procedure in paragraph 190 of the terms and conditions of services for hospital doctors.

The priority should be to try to obtain a system whereby money can follow the patient without too much bureaucracy. This used to happen in the past, but two years too late and at unrealistic standardised cost. Independent providers want extracontractual referrals, but at the moment there is no national system or dataset to deal with them. I suggest that there should be a standard system of "costings" — with a series of bandings if necessary — but based on marginal rather than total costs. The same should happen to tertiary extracontractual referrals, but the bill should go to the referring hospital rather than to the original purchaser; these again should be based on marginal cost bandings rather than full costs.

I accept the increasing power of the general practitioner as a proxy for the patient, but I'm sure that health authorities will remain the key purchasers of health care. If this is the case then they must find ways of getting closer to the patients they serve. The purchasing power of fundholders is limited at present; it would not be sensible to allow them to purchase over the whole range or planning will become extremely difficult.

Teaching and teaching hospitals

I'm very concerned about the current loss of parity for clinical academic staff but believe that the problem may be resolved again, for this year at least. An alternative would be for the university to pay the academic salary and the NHS to top up the pay for clinical work.

The service increment for teaching and research (SIFTR) is like Humpty Dumpty in *Alice Through The Looking Glass*. The calculation, which is based on the average cost per case in teaching hospitals and district general hospitals (the allocation being based on the number of medical students) is dominated by the costs in London and has much less to do with teaching and research than the high cost of running NHS estates in London.

Coopers and Lybrand are currently considering what are the measurable and legitimate extra costs of running teaching hospitals. This will be extremely important work as the SIFTR contribution currently dwarfs the Universities Funding Council's contribution to teaching at a hospital like Guy's.

The London problem

The task is to educate medical students according to best service practice, and the new curriculum at the United Medical and Dental Schools looks to the total resources available including access to many other hospitals. But it is difficult to organise any curriculum when the hospital is moving from one crisis to another. I believe that the sooner the London problem is resolved the better because it is difficult to have any real sort of planning horizon.

There may need to be an all London planning consortium which

61

seeks to determine exactly how many and which hospitals are needed in London; this must include the special health authorities. Hospitals exist to serve their local population and, whatever the trends are supposed to be, population density remains high in London; communications around London are radial so all routes lead into London and the capital development costs of moving elsewhere are very high, so that having large teaching hospitals in London will continue to make sense and need to be funded.

1 Toynbee P. The patient and the NHS. *Lancet* 1984; i: 1399-1401.

Matching resources with needs

HARRY KEEN, *chairman, NHS Support Federation*

Assessment of need

Ascertainment of need should be a major priority, separated from planning for provision of care. Nevertheless district planning must recognise and define need; this planning should be medically led.

Personally, I favour a resource management initiative both for hospitals and, in an extended and modified form, for care in the community. Goals should be set by health professionals with public input. Managers should see their role as supporting those who have to deal directly with patients rather than directing them. In Guy's hospital there was enthusiasm for clinical directorates, but now that Guy's is managed by a management board the clinical directors have been distanced from the centre and the feeling of professional ownership is gone. Clinical directors now work for managers rather than vice versa.

Research

I'd like to see the breakdown of the barriers between community medicine and hospitals. Consultants should be prepared to consult in the community, and there should be more community based research — for instance, to encourage diabetes care centres in the community. Indeed, there should be a significant increase in spending on research within the NHS. Professor Michael Peckham, the NHS director of research and development, should have a special health authority and there should be peer review for research allocations throughout the service. Sound NHS research and evaluation of procedures will improve clinical practice.

Accountability

I'm keen to see some devolution of accountability and control, with more power being devolved to regions — that is, following the model of devolution to Scotland, Wales, and Northern Ireland. Health strategy and targets would be better primarily organised at regional level as much organisation at district level is being fragmented.

Funding

The NHS is clearly underfunded and needs new money, but this should be fed into the service in stages where there is a clearly defined need. I'm not really keen on the idea of money following the patient, although I accept the need to avoid the efficiency trap; marginal costs could follow. I can see few benefits in general practitioner budget holding: although decisions on spending are taken near the patient and there *appears* to be some flexibility, in fact there is tight cash limiting. Decisions will be partly made for general practitioners or general practitioner consortia by financial managers. Where is overall policy made? There are questions about the cost of establishing general practitioner fundholding. Wouldn't more comprehensive waiting list information for each hospital and each consultant be much cheaper to provide and a more useful and effective way of reducing waiting lists, and be more likely to preserve equity?

Conclusion

Regions and districts should be assessing need and, in parallel, doing an inventory of resources to enable them to meet that need (including manpower, materials, and finance). The two could be matched through redeployment to meet need and prioritisation for additional funding. An inventory of resources could be done through health professionals in hospitals, public health departments, and, possibly, with advice from "health councils" with representation from the many health related sectors, on a district by district basis.

Being prepared and the value of non-clinical audit

BRENDAN DEVLIN, *secretary*, *National Confidential Enquiry into Perioperative Deaths*

Effectiveness

The profession must ensure that any treatment given is effective and safe. The view of many NHS managers is that consultants who consistently practice outmoded surgical techniques should be banned. There are already moves towards the "credentialing" of consultants, which would limit the scope of surgical activity and in fact prescribe particular techniques. It is important that any such changes are controlled within the profession and improvement secured through peer pressure.

Various groups are preparing guidelines for good practice which will act as standards. In addition, there should be increased opportunities for postgraduate education to enable doctors to keep up to date. Specialist registers will ensure the "correct doctor" attends the patient, but there will then be a need for recertification and special opportunities for recertification for surgeons who are found wanting. I would prefer all these measures to be overseen by the royal colleges rather than managers. The Royal College of Surgeons is interested in these topics.

Outcomes

Producing data on outcomes is a major research challenge. Outcomes are less important in terms of life and death or recurrence and non-recurrence of tumours; it is more important to look at potential disability, distress, and pain, together with patient satisfaction. Good communication skills are also vital for doctors, both for working with patients and with colleagues.

Need

I strongly believe that need can be defined. We are tied to thresholds for care — that is, at what stage in their illness should a patient have a particular treatment? The problem is that thresholds for different treatments fluctuate wildly around the country. If they could be more closely defined then it would be much easier to assess need. In the Northern region the prostatectomy rate ranges from 52 to 160/100 000. It does not require a doctor to review figures such as these and to ask why there is so much variation.

Audit

We need a much better ongoing review of clinical practice. This must depend on better universal information in the NHS. The Royal College of Surgeons has a Confidential Comparative Audit Service to enable surgeons to compare their work. The Confidential Enquiry into Perioperative Deaths (CEEPOD) now involves most surgeons in England, Wales, and Northern Ireland. The Royal College of Surgeons also accredits units for teaching, research, and clinical practice.

The college is keen to encourage the King's Fund in its organisational audit scheme. This scheme should become independent and free standing.

There is an opportunity for the profession with this sort of audit because when facilities rather than medical practice are found wanting there will be an extremely strong argument for targeted funding. I am sure that audit is one of the great successes stemming from the health service reforms.

Consultant contracts

I believe that there may need to be some form of performance related pay to act as an incentive for good practice, but I recognise that such a scheme would be difficult to manage. I would also like to break the tradition where consultants, once appointed, remain in the same place for the rest of their working lives. Why can't there be more encouragement for consultants to move around more to gain different types of experience?

It may be, in future, that not all hospital doctors need to through the same hoops for accreditation. For instance, the surgeon who wishes only to operate on hernias or varicose veins might not need to go through the full surgical training including a senior registrar post. The same system would apply to general practitioners who wish to be accredited for routine surgery of this sort. I believe that more consultants should be prepared to consult outside major hospitals but also that more general practitioners might be prepared to work in accident and emergency departments, running attached but quite distinct primary care clinics to cater for the 60% of patients who attend accident and emergency departments but need only non-emergency primary care.

Mental health

JIM BIRLEY, *consultant psychiatrist, Bethlem Royal and Maudsley Hospitals, London*

Assessment of need

For many years psychiatrists worked for, and within, defined catchment areas. They have a long tradition of thinking about the needs of a defined population. There is a considerable body of knowledge about the epidemiology of common psychiatric disorders, in terms of incidence and prevalence, and of some of the variables which affect their rates. Only recently has the thinking on the theory and methods of needs assessment become more sophisticated. Archie Cochrane maintained that if there was no treatment for a condition, there was little point in demonstrating need, except for research. The difficulty with this is that treatment is seen as something that produces a "health gain" — the unit of measurement of most current outcome research. This puts "care" below the level of treatment. But a lot of therapeutic activity is care — that is, the prevention of deterioration and the maintenance of the best level of functioning and comfort. These outcomes need to be given the same weight as health gains, both in terms of research and in thinking about needs in general, because there is already a huge burden of people with chronic or relapsing illness to be cared for and treated in all specialties of medicine. If this is not addressed the burden will press on the equally important "acute services" and impair their efficiency.

Prioritisation

Mental illness and handicap have been "priority services" for many years. While appreciating the sympathetic advice and help of many people in the Department of Health, I have to say that the proportion of money spent on our services compared with other hospital specialties has not increased. Has "prioritisation," like "treatment," prevented deterioration? To some extent our priorities have been defined by the gradual rundown of the psychiatric hospitals. Our first priority is to provide a service for the people who have been looked after by those hospitals in the past — the severely mentally ill of all ages. But we have many other pressing demands for our services.

I am in favour of a population based setting of priorities and it is up to psychiatrists to argue the case, based on the considerable amount of data which is already available. At the same time all other interested parties must be consulted and given opportunites to make recommendations, which could be both about the priorities, in terms of target populations, and about the quality and style of the services themselves. We are, however, starting from a very low level of professional and public knowledge. Many directors of public health are not giving any priority to psychiatric services, to judge by their reports. Some people in positions of power still seem to believe that mental illness is an invention of psychiatrists. The term may be invented, but what it attempts to describe and delineate is all too real. The views of sufferers and carers must thus be given a lot of weight.

Community care

I am extremely anxious about the ability of local authorities to cope in terms of finance and skills with the new arrangements coming into force in 1993. The government has pressed them too hard. Social services and social workers have many other responsibilites and priorities and there is a real danger that psychiatric services, patients, and their relatives will be marginalised. I appreciate the concern about the enormous rise in Department of Social Security payments for residential care; nevertheless, it is ironic that the government has closed down the one example of "the money following the patient" — one of the many slogans and panaceas trumpeted in *Working for Patients.*[1]

I understand that one health authority in Manchester has appointed a single manager to look after both health and residential community services. This seems an enlightened move, and more managerial and financial links between health and social services might develop in the future.

In terms of developing the complex networks of care which are

69

required to provide a community based service, these, in my view, are only just starting, both in terms of organisation and of skills. The training and activities of community psychiatric nurses are being reconsidered and, no doubt, the same reappraisals are required for other professionals, including psychiatrists. Some interesting and effective systems of care have been developed at home and abroad, and such developments in the United Kingdom will be a growth area in the next few years provided the serious shortage of low cost housing is given urgent attention.

Another possible distortion may come from fundholding practices. When such fundholding extends to all hospital provision, rather than cold surgery, how will this effect the functioning of "shared care," one of the basic approaches in psychiatry, geriatrics, and many other specialties? Will day care — a cornerstone for services for the seriously mentally ill of all ages — and home visits by hospital and day care staff be jointly paid for?

Quality

It should be possible, for most medical and psychiatric conditions, to provide patients and their carers with a checklist of what should be provided for their care by the NHS and social services. Such schedules, which are indicative rather than prescriptive, have been prepared for a number of conditions requiring shared care, such as diabetes, asthma, and hypertension. Such schedules, written in plain language, should be widely available, both to professionals and the public.

A major problem is going to be the quality of care that is going to be provided in isolated institutions, of which, ironically, there will be more rather than less with the advent of community care. These include nursing homes, sheltered accommodation, and hostels under private or statutory management which are looking after difficult and vulnerable groups of people — the old, frail, and demented; difficult and deprived children or adolescents; and some mentally ill or handicapped people. There seems to be a major problem of quality control in such places. Any professional connected with such institutions must be extremely vigilant for signs of neglect or abuse. Doctors have an ethical duty to report such matters and they should be supported, not punished, for doing so.

1 Secretaries of State for Health, Wales, Northern Ireland, and Scotland. *Working for patients*. London: HMSO, 1990. (Cmnd 555.)

Management at arm's length

PADDY ROSS, *chairman, BMA's Joint Consultants Committee*

Funding

I believe that demand is potentially infinite while resources are finite, but the government's view that there is sufficient money in the system now is wrong. One of the good things about workload related funding agreements (I do not like the term "contracts") is that need and unmet need will become more apparent — that is, it will become more clear that for this quantum of finance this quantum of "health" can be obtained. In general, however, I believe that the marketplace ethos is totally inappropriate — the evidence from the United States screams that a market is the wrong mechanism when there is finite resource.

The service is there to meet need, but it does not necessarily have to meet demand; however, if the need is met there is bound to be an increase in demand. The public health consultants must take the lead in identifying health need, and capitation based funding should also have a "need" weighting. The profession has a responsibility to become involved and also to support and promote the key role of the public health doctors.

Prioritisation

There are different approaches to prioritisation, whether it be the Oregon surveys or quality adjusted life years (QALYs). These are fine in theory, but at the end of the day it will be crucial for general practitioners and consultants to continue to weigh priority on an individual patient's clinical basis. There is also a need to be more sophisticated; having a national target for waiting times is not sensible when for patients in need of coronary artery bypass grafting

71

a wait any longer than, say, 6-9 months could lead to death, whereas for a patient with bunions waiting two years has no life threatening consequences at all.

At national and regional level there should be priority strategies which allow funding agreements for particular treatments, for instance coronary artery bypass grafting. At present this type of treatment takes place depending on available money rather than being planned on the basis of unmet need.

On the basis of national strategies and local need — assessed by directors of public health taking into account deprivation, age profiles, etc — a health authority purchaser can then prioritise blocks of money for, say, 300 coronary artery bypass grafting operations and 30 transplantations over the coming year. This broad brush approach, however, must then be finely tuned through feedback from general practitioners and, particularly, consultant providers.

Role of consultants

I am extremely worried about the levels of morale and potential recruitment in the hospital service. Some managers seem to want to give all the responsibility (for example, for costs) to consultants but are not prepared to give them any authority or power. I'm convinced that clinical directorates, which encourage consultant participation in management, must be supported. In Winchester the consultants are undoubtedly better informed about what they do, but it is too early to say whether, as a result, patients are actually getting better care. If resource management follows then the doctors can be involved in the implementation and feel some ownership; it is vital to have good clinically related information system support.

Accountability

One of the problems is that it is almost impossible to get a true representative voice of the consumer, as everybody is a consumer. Certainly the old health authority system needed review, not least because of the party political involvement. There should be representatives of various groups who have their roots in the community — for instance, community health councils.

In terms of central accountability I'm generally in favour of devolving management, but accountability must remain with the politicians. There should be broad guidelines promulgated down the management line but a measure of freedom allowed at each level to encourage local initiative.

Purchaser-provider concept

Self governing trusts

I'm not keen on self governing trusts, but I do believe that all hospitals should be managed more at arm's length from health authorities — that is, be connected by an umbilical cord or a long extendable dog lead. The concern about trusts is that they will either sink or swim entirely on their own capabilities, whereas if they have an umbilical cord action can be taken before they get into too much trouble. I'm worried that there is no real control of trusts; if one folds financially either the secretary of state will have to close it or pump money in, which would be the worst type of crisis management.

Fundholding

I am wholly against the concept of fundholding practices for three reasons. Firstly, because health authorities are charged with developing a health strategy for their local population but then the money will be taken off them and devolved to general practitioners, who may have a completely different approach. Secondly, giving general practitioners the money to buy hospital services could lead to them purchasing the cheapest option (that is, quality could suffer), and then it is the general practitioners who keep the savings whereas in the past the hospital kept the saving if it performed well, which could then be reinvested in better facilities. Thirdly, currently 87% of the work of the Royal Hampshire hospital comes from the Winchester Health Authority and a further percentage from other surrounding health authorities. With the increasing number of fundholders, however, the hospital could have 200 different contracts, which would be a bureaucratic nightmare. How can the hospital hope to monitor these and plan its services sensibly?

Referrals

There must be clinical freedom for general practitioners to refer where they like. The district health authority (assuming that the family health services authorities become merged with district health authorities) should *monitor* referral patterns, and if Dr X routinely

73

sends all his patients who need a hip operation out of the district they should ask why. I find the whole idea of extracontractual referrals appalling, just a method of applying strict cash limits.

I believe that money should follow the patient quickly and with the minimum bureaucracy. At present it is the financial system which is controlling referrals. In fact, the vast majority of contracts are of the block type so money is *not* following the patient, so most hospitals are still, effectively, cash limited. This is bound to lead to financial problems for a number of trusts as the year progresses because purchasers are trying to get as many patients into the block contracts as they can. Most providers would like to move on to cost or volume contracts as soon as they can, but at present most of the information systems are totally inadequate.

Hospital provision

Beds

I am not convinced that there will be a decreased need for hospital beds over the coming years. Emergency admissions are actually increasing — at the Royal Hampshire, for instance, admissions have gone up by about 80% over the past 10 years whereas the number of beds has dropped by 15%. The population has not increased significantly over that timespan. The increase in acute admissions particularly puts pressure on elective surgery. Day surgery is fine, but a critical mass of inpatient beds is required for acute admissions and elective work. I believe that the only part of the NHS with too many beds is probably London.

Integration

I like the idea of a seamless service. There should be less need for follow up in hospital if there is better dialogue between consultants and general practitioners. Diabetes, for instance, could be dealt with in a much more integrated manner; there could also be national advisory protocols produced by the royal colleges. I'm not very keen on increasing the amount of consultant outreach work — for example, in health centres — unless it can be organised to be cost effective; consultants must ensure effective use of available resources.

Performance

I accept that there are significant variations in professional performance but believe that the clinical directorate concept will prove to be good for dealing particularly with poor contractual performance — that is, through peer review; the system will also be useful for encouraging medical audit. I'm concerned, however, about there being too rigid an approach to performance indicators such as standard throughputs in outpatient departments and operating theatres; it is only natural that different specialties and different individuals move at different paces.

It must be the individual doctor's responsibility to keep up to date, but peer review or pressure may have to be applied in some cases. It is quite acceptable for managers to ask questions but the profession should see it is done. I'm not keen on individual financial incentives for continuing medical education in the hospital service; doctors should want to keep up to date as part of their professional upbringing. I know, however, that the Royal College of Obstetricians, for instance, is introducing a points system for attending training courses; obstetricians will have to recertify every five years and, if not recertified, would not be accredited as being specialist in the Medial Register.

Medical education

I believe that there are too many medical schools in London and that the distinction which continues to be drawn between teaching and non-teaching hospitals is daft. Teaching is now done in practically all hospitals, so the nomenclature should be changed to "university hospitals" and "district general hospitals." Medical students should spend time at both types of hospital, particularly in outpatient departments, but also in general practices. I believe, however, that medical education should still be based in a hospital, preferably a centre of excellence.

Research

Research within the NHS must be protected, but I'm against the idea that junior doctors have to do a stack of research to enable them to be appointed as a consultant. I believe that the "amateurs" need exposure to research and research method but that it is the professional high flyers who should be really encouraged and facilitated. A medical degree is not absolutely necessary to do medical research, and I would encourage more use of people with PhDs, for instance.

Consultants' performance and counterproductive incentives

JOHN CHAWNER, *chairman, BMA's Central Consultants and Specialists Committee*

Performance

I accept that there are apparent differences in consultants' performance around the country but query whether this is actually a problem. International comparisons show that the United Kingdom has a high standard of secondary care and there are remarkably few complaints given the number of consultant and patient episodes. Nevertheless, appreciable differences should be investigated, although this should be done only through peer review.

I'm not very happy about the concept of reaccrediting senior hospital staff. This will be extremely stressful; doctors in their 50s should not be threatened with further exams. I'm also unhappy about possible incentives to improve performance; I believe, for instance, that performance related pay could actually be counterproductive in drawing consultants' attention to the hours they actually work — that is, any incentives must clearly improve performance not risk worsening it. The same applies to the consultant contract — the more clinical commitments are fixed the less doctors will tend to do within that rigid framework.

There should be proper research on these issues, covering standards and performance levels. I'm convinced, however, that most consultants work over and above their contracted hours; indeed, many of the bed closures around the country have been due to too much unplanned work being done by consultants and their using up their budgets prematurely.

Clinical directorates and the resource management initiative

Clinical directorates are fine if designed along the lines of the Central Consultants and Specialists Committee (CCSC) recommendations. It is important that consultants should not just be taking on a management role for the manager but that they should actually be part of management, rather than subservient to it.

Resource management is a confusing term and nobody has yet defined what it really means. It should, however, provide management information to support the clinical decision making process. This requires a whole stack of different types of information; not all costs decisions should be made at unit level, some must be made more centrally.

Peer involvement

I do not wish to see consultants' contracts and job descriptions changing significantly. I'm aware that some consultants, once appointed, can become sidetracked into clinical work not entirely related to their original job description or the needs of the local population. This should not be allowed to happen through clinical director or peer pressure, which should ensure that all are pulling broadly in the same direction to deal with demand. Clinical colleagues will be much better able to assess the value of innovatory work than managers; I do not want a system which is so planning and resource orientated that innovation is stifled. There should be more flexibility through peer involvement rather than managerial dictat.

Purchaser-provider concept

I do not accept that the purchaser-provider principle can work in practice. I agree that under the new arrangements the purchaser should be able to determine the type and amount of care to be provided; however, purchasers are in fact asking providers to say what type of treatment they are undertaking and how much they are doing, then contracting for that. I do not accept that this might just be a function of the first year "steady state" situation. I do not believe that purchasers are ever going to be in a position to assess need except through provider units — the only people who know how many hip replacements are necessary are those who are actually doing them and who see the demand.

77

I broadly support the concept of money following the patient, but I'm concerned about moving money away from places that cannot properly compete in the "market." I would prefer a diagnosis related group (DRG) system funded by a central agency with strong professional involvement. Therefore, a consultant doing a lot of hip replacements would get a lot of money allocated for hip diagnosis related groups.

I'm not keen on the concept of QALYs (quality adjusted life years) as there might be a tendency to make decisions solely on the basis of the QALY score. I could not accept a situation where treatments with low QALY scores might not be approved. There must be more research on treatment effectiveness including patient follow up to help doctors make decisions on the priorities. I'm not happy about Oregon type prioritisation in this country; if it is shown to work in America it is possibly because Americans tend to be better informed about medicine and health issues generally.

Funding

The "bottomless pit" argument should be challenged. I'm sure that, in a market sense, there is not infinite demand. The underfunding of the health service should be tackled as a priority; it is a key political issue and the public have shown their willingness to pay more for health, not only through opinion polls but through the vast amount of money paid for patent medicines in the United Kingdom.

I'm convinced that there should be a hypothecated health tax. We need to get spending on health care up to about 9% of the gross domestic product. Some of this increase would come from the hypothecated tax and the rest of the increase should come from the private sector, which should increase its share to about 2% of the overall 9%. To enable this I would abolish the regulations preventing general practitioners from charging their own patients; this would encourage general practitioner involvement in the private sector.

This would mean that the NHS would have fewer patients to deal with, and therefore there would be more pounds per patient. I accept that the Treasury might wish to reduce NHS funds accordingly but believe that this could be prevented if the health element of taxation was hypothecated — that is, any such adjustment by the Treasury would then have to be done in an explicit manner.

I've no objection to people raising money for health care locally on a voluntary basis but do not believe that local health tax is a practical proposition.

Accountability

I'm not keen on further devolution of NHS management authority from the secretary of state to the NHS Management Executive. It is important that the secretary of state answers for deficiencies in health care for which he is responsible.

At local level I would be happier with the concept of non-executive directors of health authorities if there was less political bias in their selection (and that of health authority chairmen). I suggest that some independent body should be involved in the selection process, both of chairmen and of non-executive directors. I was not happy with the old system of health authority membership, which again was subject to political pressures and tended to lead to parochialism.

I believe that health authorities should continue to be accountable in a number of ways: through ministers, who may have to answer parliamentary questions at any time; through the accountability of the health professionals working within the authority (that is, to the General Medical Council, etc); through the law of the land; and, in part, through line management to the region.

I support the community health councils, which should perform a local watchdog role. I believe that this is to the profession's advantage and that we should be working with representatives of consumers. Like for non-executive directors, however, better selection procedures could be designed for community health council members.

Research

I'm concerned about the quality of some of the research being done, particularly by those doing research principally to build up a portfolio for a consultant appointment. I doubt whether much of this research is really necessary and question what return it gives to the health service. I hope that the new NHS research and development policy will lead to a more coordinated approach and a more sensible use of research funds.

Integration of primary and secondary care

I accept that there is likely to be a decreasing utilisation of beds (as there is in the rest of Europe) because of shorter bed stay generally and the greater emphasis on day surgery. I believe, however, that the emphasis on beds is wrong. Modern emphasis in relation to hospital care should be less on beds but more on intensive treatment and investigation.

I strongly support the need for rationalisation of hospitals, on split sites for instance, but doubt the need for a significant reduction in the number of district general hospitals. I am also doubtful about a resurgence of community hospitals as, even if they were not staffed by specialists, more consultants might be needed to provide services on a visiting basis.

Payments for skills and extra work

LORD IAN MCCOLL, *professor of surgery, United Medical and Dental Schools of Guy's and St Thomas's Hospitals*

Problems in the NHS

The problem with the system before the reforms was that there were no incentives to encourage improved performance. Hospital managements had little clue what was going on and the efficiency trap meant that less and less could be done as the year progressed. It was essential to have money following the patient immediately, not, as in the past, when money did follow the patient but two years too late and at a price that was too low for hospitals — particularly London teaching hospitals — to survive on.

There have also been real problems in the service through the absence of good managers. The surfeit of poor administrators was probably due to inadequate pay. I'm pleased that this situation is now beginning to be remedied.

Flexibility of pay

I strongly believe that national agreements on pay are a disaster for all groups, including doctors. There must be local flexibility for managers, who, if they cannot recruit good people, must be able to pay more. Health authorities need to work out their priorities and then be able to organise their remuneration packages accordingly. I do, of course, accept national agreements on minimum rates of pay.

Consultants' salaries, in relation to the overall pay bill, are peanuts, so authorities should be able to pay reasonable rates. Remuneration should be work related, so if consultants do more work in future they will be remunerated accordingly. I believe that as part of their work consultants should be encouraged to consult in the community.

Purchaser-provider concept

I think that district health authorities will be the prime purchasers and will be able to plan accordingly. In south London three district health authorities are getting together in a consortium to strengthen their purchasing power and to enable sensible planning for their areas.

NHS hospitals are now in competition with private hospitals; this may enable a cheaper service. Nevertheless, I'm strongly against privatisation of the NHS, which can come to compete on equal terms with the private sector in due course.

I'm against the prescription of a core service. Let the market decide. For instance, pressure on waiting lists will force an increase in the number of consultants in particular specialties because of the insistence by purchasers on that work being done.

I'm a strong believer in the clinical directorate system of the kind which was first promoted at Guy's Hospital and which has enabled clinical pressure to be put on managers. Resource management alone is not enough. There must be a management structure to go with it and money following the patient. Clinical directors should be paid adequately and encouraged not to leave clinical work if necessary.

Accountability

At local level representatives on health authorities have usually been a disaster, and I would include some university representatives in that statement. I'm happy with the concept of non-executive directors being appointed in their own right, some of whom are very good. I'm happy with the accountability both of health authorities and self governing trusts, which are still accountable to the secretary of state.

Teaching hospitals

In relation to the university and NHS relationship I believe that teaching hospitals should have a coordinating role. Students will have to go where the patients are, which may not be the teaching hospitals because they may not have the right case mix for teaching. Attitudes in teaching hospitals have to change both to medical students themselves, about whom most are extremely complacent, and to the role of peripheral hospitals, where a great deal of good medicine is practised.

Career structure

It is high time the distinction between registrars and senior registrars was abolished. We should be appointing consultants at the age of 32, when doctors are in their most dynamic and innovative phases; it is a complete waste of these skills to keep them waiting, frustrated, until the age of 38 or more.

Research and development

The money spent on research and development has to be justified. Is it good research? Is it valuable to the university or NHS or is it just being done to enable advancement up the career ladder? Senior academics have a key responsibility not only for research but also for teaching, for which they must be undertaking regular clinical work.

A call for definitions

W M ROSS, *secretary, Conference of Colleges, Royal College of Radiologists*

Purchaser-provider concept

Need for a pilot exercise

I perceive fundholding as the real problem because of the potential of changed demand on local hospitals through referral patterns that could change weekly depending on a variety of circumstances. It is also very complicated for health authority finance departments to have to deal with so many disparate providers. I have always argued that the implementation of the "reforms" should be slowed down and that there should be a proper pilot exercise with the key criterion for evaluation being benefit for patients.

Targets and screening

I support the concept of a health strategy but *The Health of the Nation*[1] can be only the start. For instance, it defines targets for only three cancers; there need to be targets for other cancers, such as colon, bladder, and head and neck cancers. The target of decreasing the incidence of cancers within 10 years is too short a time to make realistic judgments. In relation to screening, I am concerned about the problem of false positive results that might occur if demand goes up significantly; it will be crucial to have experts to do the screening to keep up standards, which has implications for resources, particularly of skilled staff.

Purchasing problems

Something along the lines of the purchaser-provider system has been running in Newcastle for five years now — that is, the health authority has allocated funds to units for, in effect, "block contracts." I believe that purchasers will find real problems with what precisely to purchase; I'm not convinced that total separation of purchaser and provider will be practical. At the very least purchasers must have advice in some form from local provider consultant representatives.

Standards of practice

I accept that there are wide variations in practice and performance around the country, but it is important to recognise the different standards of competence and performance that occur in any profession. The problem is to define when the standards fall into the unacceptable category, when something must be done, preferably by fellow professionals.

There is the possibility of 10 year reaccreditation for consultants, possibly through exams, though not necessarily. The only sanction that a royal college would have if a doctor chose not to "go through the hoop," however, would be to request the General Medical Council not to continue to indicate that the doctor has completed higher specialist training in the Medical Register.

Funding and costings

There needs to be a definition of what the public can expect to be provided through general taxation. Anything over and above that would have to be covered by other means — for instance, extra health insurance. I believe that if people are prepared to pay extra taxation if they know it is going to health care, then they will also be prepared to buy insurance for add on benefits. I'm sure that funding health care through general taxation is the best way, principally because it is seen to be more equitable on a national basis.

I fully acknowledge that there are inefficiencies in the service. Much better information systems were needed to help deal with this, but *not* the new management structure which has appeared on the back of it. There is still not nearly enough information on costs; in most units it is very difficult even to cost a chest x ray, taking into account true costs, overheads, etc. I can see merit in the suggestion that charging should be based on banded costs, but there would still need to be a pilot exercise to work out the bandings.

The Freeman Hospital in Newcastle has had resource management for five years now, but they still have only just got it into the outpatient department and it is not yet installed on all the wards.

Without costing or at least bandings it is really impossible to run block contracts, never mind the rather more complicated extracontractual referrals.

Education and training

It is vitally important to have an educational structure which enables teaching and examination in specialist fields. I therefore believe it is self evident that there must continue to be teaching hospitals and royal colleges (most hospitals now do some teaching, so "teaching hospital" may be a misnomer).

Combined Department of Health and university support for teaching hospitals has been valuable over the years and the flexible "knock for knock" agreements have done a great deal to allow standards to be maintained.

Conclusion

I believe that there needs to be a definition of health followed by a definition of a health service — from this it might be possible to calculate what the government should be trying to fund.

1 Secretary of State for Health. *The health of the nation*. London: HMSO, 1991. (Cm 1523.)

Cost conciousness and failure of the advisory structure

ANGUS FORD, *chairman, BMA's Scottish Council*

Cost effectiveness

I believe that the reforms came because the NHS was seen as a bottomless pit in relation to funding. We must argue for targeted funds. The NHS has to get in place a system which is semi-predictable, makes people accountable at local level, and in which all are clearly conscious of the costs of their actions.

If the money is not there the system just will not work. I accept that no country can satisfy all health demand, but funding arguments will be stronger if there is clearly value for money provided within the service. Professionals must be able to justify treatments and investigations and, for their part, politicians have to try to understand the pressures put on health professionals through their direct contact with patients.

There is a problem in "controlling" the spending of junior staff; control mechanisms are needed that do not suppress initiative but that are ever mindful of the need for cost effectiveness. There are already prescribing formularies, for instance; perhaps there could also be investigation formularies. Managers have to understand, however, that junior staff may need to spend more on investigations than consultants.

I'm in favour of clinical directorates and resource management, but so far there has been no resource management in Scotland because managers see billing systems as the current priority.

I'm not too unhappy about consultants being given broad targets by purchasing authorities. It might be useful for a consultant to know that he has to do, say, 300 hip replacements next year; at least he will have a planning horizon and can plan his time accordingly. But there must be feedback from consultants as providers to purchasers.

Medical advice

I believe that the statutory advisory structure has singularly failed in its principal task to give objective advice on what should be the best medical approaches for our patients. Often medical advisory committees have been categorised more by geographical and specialty vested interests and frank self interest. This is as much a central problem as a local problem. The profession has discredited its own advisory structure; "advisors" have to be doctors in whom their colleagues have confidence, and the profession has to accept a degree of management input. I'm convinced that management will just select their "good guys" if the profession does not get its act together.

Performance

I'm concerned about the well known variations in doctors' performance around the country. I strongly believe that the profession should take the initiative and encourage performance appraisal for doctors; this after all is a normal management technique in most other walks of life now. Doctors should not be able to get out of it on the basis of clinical freedom because the appraisal must be done only by peer review. Clinical directors, or perhaps heads of division, would need to be properly trained to perform appraisals, would have to conduct appraisals in an informal non-threatening manner, and would have to make it clear that the appraisal had no connection with pay or merit award. This will not be easy but it is a mettle which has to be grasped before managers take it on themselves.

Purchaser-provider concept

Identification of needs

One of the good things about the purchaser-provider concept is that purchasers should identify needs. This will be a function of the director of public health but must include advice from clinicians. This then will dictate the purchasing pattern. I'm concerned at the apparent failure of local community health councils because that a watchdog is needed is part of the citizen's or patient's charter; perhaps a new watchdog could be launched (entitled something like "Health Watch") with a more defined role. One of the functions would be to liaise with the director of public health with relation to purchasing policy.

Self governing trusts

In many hospitals there has been a hankering for greater autonomy from health boards (district health authorities) and a feeling that the old boards of management were no bad thing. The real problem with self governing trusts is the management freedom to vary pay and terms and conditions of service, particularly for consultants. Where possible pressure should be put on trust managements at least to ensure national minimums for pay and basic terms and conditions of service. There is already great flexibility within senior hospital doctors' terms and conditions — for instance, to appoint half way up the scale or to offer extra notional half days. This sort of flexibility should be encouraged rather than a complete wrecking of national agreements.

Fundholding

I'm not happy with fundholding, but at least there are properly evaluated pilot projects taking place in Scotland. I believe that fundholders should be able to purchase only under the umbrella of health strategies and targets set up by the purchasing authorities and their directors of public health.

Hospital provision

I'm keen to encourage more integration between primary and secondary care, particularly in my specialty of paediatrics. It is also important to reduce the confusion over who covers what and at what time. I'm not convinced that "consulting" in the community is cost effective. I can see an increased need for shared care — for instance, in diabetes, cystic fibrosis, and asthma — but perhaps it would be more cost effective for specialist staff grade doctors to be involved in this on a day to day basis. I certainly support the concept of community hospitals, particularly in Scotland, where there are many isolated areas where access to major district general hospitals is difficult.

In fact, this is one of the reasons why there is an apparent difference in funding between Scotland and England, but, after geography, different rating systems, different funding of ambulance services, etc, is taken into account, the difference amounts to more like 9% than the 25% promoted by some. I accept, however, that health care is probably seen as better in Scotland not least because of the much reduced use of private practice; English levels should be brought up to the Scottish levels rather than vice versa.

Need for more information technology

RUSSELL HOPKINS, *chairman, BMA's Welsh Council Unit, and former general manager, University Hospital of Wales*

Inefficiency

A key issue for the NHS is that budgets or money accrued to the hospitals should be work related. The previous arrangement of providing a hospital with a finite sum of money meant that if it achieved greater productivity the money ran out more quickly; this was self defeating — the hospital was strangled by its success. There has been considerable waste of resources in the past and there continues to be waste, although this is improving. The increased efficiency would not have been achieved were it not for Mrs Thatcher's financial squeeze on the NHS. The NHS is basically underfunded and, particularly, the hospital service has never had the capital investment required. With little planned maintenance or replacement of equipment most hospitals have considerable reservoirs of debt and repeated funding crises as a result of equipment breakdown.

Management

I am convinced that when doctors are in managerial control of their clinical services they work harder and have increased motivation, but this has to happen in a well managed environment. Overall, I do not believe that many consultants are interested in actively involving themselves in general management but many will be prepared to take on managerial responsibilities in clinical directorates. I am a keen supporter of both the resource management initiative and clinical directorates, but consultants must assume the responsibility and accountability that goes with them. Management is different from running a department.

I remain convinced that senior consultants could and should play a major part in general management — this could be a sideways move in the latter part of a clinical career.

Flexible pay systems

It is vital that money follows the patient and that the internal market works. This means a type of piecework system, but I would be against an item of service pay for senior doctors. This can easily become a treadmill of diminishing returns. In addition to money being paid to hospitals for work done, I believe there must be local responsibility for costs rather than rigid national agreements — that is, there should be local flexibility. In this context self governing trusts do have the flexibility to pay more for those working harder. I believe that some hospital doctors, particularly consultants, have for too long been able to satisfy their own professional interests rather than what their NHS patients require. Doctors must think of their patients as people and all hospital staff remember that hospitals are there because of their patients, not because of the staff.

Information technology

Self governing trusts have more flexibility than directly managed units and they are free of the district health authority bureaucracy. They will be more efficient as a result. However, there is a real problem with lack of data and information systems and the inadequate investment and NHS expertise in these.

The first approach to bringing in information technology is to find out what the managers and the professionals actually need; only then can the hardware and software be purchased. I believe that the NHS and self governing trusts are short of managers who are properly trained to deal with information systems, financial experts, and the information technology itself. I acknowledge that managing hospitals and units is extremely difficult at present and managers must spend more money on administration. The enlarged administration must deliver and be efficient otherwise unit general managers will inevitably find themselves going into the red and the clinicians will become even more disaffected.

Accountability

Managers

I believe that most managers are as dedicated and committed to the welfare of the NHS and its patients as anybody else, including doctors. I believe there are many good people in NHS management but not enough. The further they work away from the patient and clinical pressures the less valuable they are, and the less they understand problems and the need to take decisions. Consultants can become good general managers who are not afraid of taking decisions.

Data collection

Audit, NHS contracts, and clinical services will eventually have the information technology data collection systems to cover most of their needs; nevertheless, there will still be a need to win the clinicians' cooperation and persuade them to put a clear diagnosis in the notes or correct code on a computer sheet. There must be a continuous audit of hospital notes. If clinicians have their own budget and the notes cannot be coded there will be financial sanctions largely of their own making. The clinicians must "own" the system and see that it is in their own interest to make it work.

Core service

In relation to a possible core service I believe that patients should pay towards the hospital hotel charges; all patients should make a significant contribution, the clinical treatment being free at the point of delivery to the patient.

Local accountability

I believe that the non-executive directors should take part in strategic decisions only. Establishing a good medical advisory system would be a gain, but I believe quite reasonable advice will be available through the directorate system, which will strengthen the position of doctors in the NHS.

Teaching and research

Although the benefits of the continued relationship between the NHS and academia are considerable, there are difficulties. The saying "absence of professors" has not come about for nothing, and professors' influence on distinction awards, development of clinical services, and staff appointments is considerable and not always desirable. The symbiotic relationship between the NHS and academia is significantly weighted in favour of academia. Teaching hospitals will have major problems competing in the "new world" if distinction awards, often awarded for non-hands on clinical achievement, are to be included in the contract price. National institutions or the Department of Health may have to be cross charged to cover the absence of such staff.

I am not too sure about the value of Michael Peckham's research and development initiative for the NHS, but I do believe that a doctor who has a major time commitment to research should be employed by a university rather than the NHS.

Time for management

JOHN HALLIDAY, *former chairman, BMA's Northern Ireland Council*

Funding

Funding in Northern Ireland has traditionally been better than in England, although it has decreased comparatively since the start of direct rule from London. As in Scotland, there is less private practice in Northern Ireland than in England; this is thought to be due in part to the generally better funding and in part to socioeconomic factors, particularly high unemployment in the province.

I believe that the country can afford to fund a comprehensive national health service. Indeed, it can't afford not to have an NHS as anything else would be more expensive. Equity of health care must be offered as far as possible, although I accept that some of the more expensive treatements may have to be restricted.

Clinical directorates

The reforms will not begin to take effect in Northern Ireland until April 1992. I support the concept of clinical directorates, but I'm concerned that clinical directors have to do the work essentially in their own time. I'm also concerned about inadequate back up resources, particularly inadequate information and administrative support. Doctors must be involved in management but have to be allocated proper time — at least two notional half days would seem appropriate.

The need for a notional half day a week for medical audit, together with the juniors' concern about absentee trainers, whether for academic or management reasons, makes the argument for increasing the number of consultants even more compelling.

Performance

I believe that some consultants are badly organised administratively; they need to stand back and look at what they do. Doctors are being paid by an employer, who has to be satisfied with performance and work load. The average consultant, however, works more than he or she is contracted to and, if management tries to screw consultants down to any great extent, they could end up working to contract, which could have an extremely detrimental long term effect.

Accountability

Under the old arrangements it was very difficult to get real decisions out of the health board. I accept that the new system is less democratic but at least decisions are now being made. Nevertheless, health boards should be answerable to a wider body annually. I do not believe there is anything to fear from consumerism.

One of the difficulties is to draw a line between medical responsibility and social responsibility. Doctors and managers should be working together to develop a broad approach to planning.

Community care

There is general support in Northern Ireland for health boards which combine health and social services. The structure at least recognises how difficult it is to divorce physical and medical and social needs. There are some concerns about the size of the responsibility and the difficulties of coordination; nevertheless, I believe that it must be more cost effective to run both services under one umbrella. There are, however, continuing funding problems and worries that much of the finance which should be targeted at health seems to be going into the social services.

Conclusion

In summary, I believe that the number one objective is to maintain and strengthen the current NHS, although I would be prepared to consider a system such as that used in Denmark, where there is at least an element of personal responsibility gained in part through charging. We must always be striving to make the service more efficient; this will mean identifying and eliminating waste, increasing the work load of some staff, and, importantly, decreasing the work load of other staff so that they can be more effective in what they seek to do.

Rethinking education

ELIZABETH SHORE, *dean of postgraduate medical education, North West Thames Regional Health Authority*

Education

Both undergraduate and postgraduate education in this country need a long cool rethink. Undergraduate education has become ossified. I'm not convinced that hospitals are necessarily the right place to train doctors. I am concerned about the General Medical Council's consultation document on the undergraduate medical curriculum as there seems to be an acceptance that medical schools can no longer produce a rounded doctor at qualification. The royal colleges may, as a result, want to increase even further the time spent in formal postgraduate training.

I would like to see more medical students being taught in the community, but there will be real problems with this. I believe that the general practitioner training system is excellent, but there will be problems of space in surgeries and there will almost certainly also need to be a new supervisory system to maintain standards.

Teaching hospitals are having to farm out their students over increasingly long distances. I think that the teaching hospitals themselves do not know where they are going. Are they centres for tertiary referrals and research or are they teaching centres? If they are teaching centres then they must have a good case mix. Will this happen with some of the teaching hospital trusts in London — for instance, those that seem more interested in getting patients from overseas than London itself?

Research

Research is grossly underfunded at present, particularly health service research. If, as Michael Peckham, the new director of research and development, aims, the NHS research and development budget is going to be 1.5% of the whole, then coordination of research within the NHS will be a key priority. Independent bodies such as the Medical Research Council will also continue to be extremely important and there should be close cooperation and dialogue with them.

Research does not necessarily have to be done primarily in teaching hospitals. Research and development money should be used for research into effectiveness of treatment in district general hospitals and, perhaps, some of it could be used to buy research sessions for consultants in these hospitals, all of whom will have have had research experience to have been appointed as consultants. An alternative would be for some of the money to be used for consultants to take sabbaticals to pursue their clinical research interests.

Audit

I believe that medical audit should be seen as part of postgraduate education and that most postgraduate deans would support this. In some regions there is a parallel audit structure outside the postgraduate channels, but there should be much more collaborative work and effort put into the educational aspects of audit. I find it extraordinary that an extra £5.8m was put into postgraduate education in 1991-2 in England but over the same time £48.6m was put into medical audit. If there isn't coordination of these two programmes inside the Department of Health there is little wonder there isn't coordination at regional level.

In relation to health promotion, I believe that the expertise needed for this is probably more educational than medical. Health promotion really needs to be started in schools as part of the national curriculum, and I wonder whether it would not be better covered by the Department of Education and Science.

Manpower

I believe that we may not need to increase numbers of general practitioners any further if the primary care team is built up further and if nurses take on more of a role in primary care. I accept that there is a need to maintain or possibly increase the number of career posts because most medical students quite naturally are aiming to become consultants or general practitioners.

I suggest that a distinction could be drawn between "super" consultants and "specialists." The more senior grade could be comparatively small and consist of medical managers and clinical directors, consultants undertaking tertiary or quaternary referrals, and consultants involved in organising education. The rest would be named specialists, but after say 10 years many would begin to seek super consultant posts. These would be advertised and appointed through open competition. Specialists could be appointed at a younger age than at present. The system would have the advantage of encouraging more geographical movement among consultants, who currently tend to get stuck from the age of their consultant appointment onwards. The higher grade could be paid for, at least in part, by funds from the merit award budget.

The need for an academic training

COLIN SMITH, *chairman, BMA's Medical Academic Staff Committee*

Medical schools

Medical education must never become a technical training exercise. The threat of this is very real, at least in part because of the suggestion that there should be only five or six major research centres in the United Kingdom. The university sector traditionally provides specialist expertise; this *can* be provided by others but is often left to the academics as they tend to be at the advancing edge of medicine. It is important to understand that medicine has an intellectual base beyond that of singular vocational training and needs to be serviced through a broad university education; I therefore believe strongly that medical education should stay under the auspices of the Department of Education and Science, with the responsibility shared with the Department of Health.

I am extremely concerned about the currrent, hopefully temporary, loss of parity for clinical academic staff. There is a need to review the fundamental relationships between universities and the NHS but not to destroy the platform on which they are built. Ideally all funds for clinical academic staff should come from the universities, but there might increasingly need to be a greater input from the NHS towards medical education. The interface between medical schools and the NHS is currently being studied by the France committee, which accepts that the NHS must have some say in academic matters and vice versa.

Teaching hospitals

Involvement of medical schools should be with more than just the teaching hospitals. The service increment for teaching and research

101

(SIFTR) is not just paid in relation to undergraduate education but also in relation to postgraduate education of registrars, senior registrars, etc. Teaching hospitals have a critical mass of specialist services, and are at the leading edge of medical research.

Should the nature of teaching hospital consultant appointments be changed to reflect the nature of the interface between the medical school and the NHS? There could be joint appointment of all teaching hospital consultants by the university and the NHS with the work required for each sector carefully negotiated in advance. This would help to make a teaching hospital truly a university hospital and could encourage more "independence" of teaching hospitals.

I accept the General Medical Council's proposals that more student teaching should be done in the primary care sector in future. I strongly believe, however, that structured teaching will still be necessary as medical education is not just about common disease. For instance, it will be extremely difficult to get enough suitable patients to learn how to perform neurological examination in general practice; general practice training, however, is excellent for under-standing patient care and disease within the community. In addition, the interface between research and medical education is vital. Research teaches students to question, to investigate, and to seek outcomes and answers; this is an extremely important attitudinal approach which is crucial to medicine generally.

Research

I welcome the attempt by Michael Peckham, the NHS director of research and development, to ensure that research and development takes up 1.5% of the NHS budget. I'm extremely concerned, however, at the suggestion that this research and development budget should include, for instance, costs of postgraduate education. Postgraduate education must be funded separately to fulfil the requirements of the service to the community. If there are no funds there will not be the necessary maintenance of skills to run a safe service.

I think it is important for doctors in training to undertake clinical research. It gives a discipline of thought and an understanding of the limitations of medicine which cannot be achieved by any other process. It is important for young doctors to realise that just because a belief is held that does not mean it is true; if doctors are given a problem they should address the real problem rather than just the symptoms — that is, they should try to think laterally or use "knight's move" thinking.

I do not believe there is a great deal of evidence to show that research money is being wasted on useless research. Nevertheless we should develop a discipline that research is not done with the aim of improving curriculum vitae but to gain a better educational and clinical approach to medicine; this may mean that the emphasis of research will have to be changed. At Southampton Medical School students do a project or study in depth for over eight months; most of them undertake a research topic, including a literature review, on anything from pure laboratory studies to projects in alternative medicine, and produce a mini thesis. This type of early approach to research concepts should be encouraged in other schools.

Funding of research

Within two years universities will have much less money to spend on research infrastructure. Infrastructure money will not be given to the Universities Funding Council in future but to the research councils. Therefore, it is likely that only those universities with top league projects will obtain funding — there will be little money to support the middle orders (that is, good but not top class research). In addition, the overheads for research will increasingly have to be covered by the grant awarding bodies, including the charities.

Michael Peckham hopes that NHS research money will be directed to fulfil the expectations of national targets. There are three areas where NHS research and development monies are likely to be used: to assess and achieve the broad targets set out in *The Health of the Nation*[1]; for research on outcomes; and for epidemiological research work. These key areas are all very well, but how will people find research money for other areas not prioritised, particularly if they are unable to get Medical Research Council grants. Research in one area may be, sometimes unwittingly, the key to a solution in another area, so there needs to be flexibility, continued innovation, and collaboration.

Regional research committees have a number of problems, particularly relating to the control of spending. They themselves have no outcome measures and little accountability. They often also have little meaningful control over projects which are being undertaken.

103

They should have the right to review projects, perhaps halfway through, and real mechanisms for assessment and control, so that funding can be stopped if necessary (as do the Medical Research Council and the Wellcome Foundation).

Purchaser-provider concept

Self governing trust teaching hospitals could have significant changes in their case mix due to contracting. The implications for teaching and the costs of alternative ways of maintaining case mix must be addressed *before* contracts are implemented. The Department of Health is responsible for providing facilities for medical education, so if changes have to be made to the curriculum or students have to travel to other hospitals appropriate funds have to be provided.

I'm not sure that the purchaser-provider concept is the best way to encourage best services and it will certainly increase the administrative costs of the service, but to what purpose? The problems could have been approached differently through resource management, medical audit, etc, but I accept that the purchaser-provider concept has sharpened the debate on quality, cost control, and cost effectiveness, and is perhaps the best we can do at present.

There is a great need to look critically at the outcome and quality of treatments but also a need to continue to ask more fundamental questions — for instance, not only should we be looking for better ways of treating cataracts, we should be looking for methods of preventing cataract formation. I'm concerned that purchasing and contracting will lead to a less questioning approach in relation to prevention and alternatives. Will the people making the purchasing decisions have the information, expertise, and questioning approach not just to repeat previous decisions and mistakes?

I'm also concerned that the purchaser-provider concept will tend to disintegrate what links there are between primary care and hospital care. It is good medicine for consultants to go out and consult in the community, although it may not be cost effective and they may be needed on site for emergency cover, but what incentives for this sort of approach will there be? Indeed, who will determine the overall nature of the service and who will be responsible for determining its quality? It is unfortunate that other measures of quality are not yet well developed and those responsible for quality assurance have often had no training in its assessment or assurance.

104

Funding

The true cost of health care is effectively hidden from the population because of the system of general taxation. An alternative, therefore, would be to be much more explicit and have a quite separate health care tax. This would increase accountability, for any increase in the tax would have to be clearly justified. If you believe in the current approach you have to accept that health will remain a political football and that the people themselves will continue to have little say or control. A hypothecated health tax, however, could lead to a reduction in funding under some circumstances. The principles of the NHS are still being followed, just, but the introduction of explicit rationing on funds is in breach of these principles.

Without funding at perhaps 2% more of gross domestic product the country clearly cannot continue to have a health system which guarantees access at any time for all. In which case the population must accept either prioritisation or continued rationing through waiting lists. In addition to seeking more money it might be possible to reduce health spending by having a radical review of the whole structure of the health service. Should we, for example, continue with the distinction between primary and secondary care? Could we develop a range of specialist centres around the country which will be accessible to all patients without general practitioner referral?

1 Secretary of State for Health. *The health of the nation*. London: HMSO, 1991. (Cm 1523.)

POLITICS AND MANAGEMENT

Offering an alternative

SAM GALBRAITH MP, *Labour Scottish Spokesman on Health*

Assessment of need

I do not accept the "bottomless pit" argument; the health service must not be based on demand but on need, and need is finite. The important thing is to try to define need by using those working on the ground. Hospitals are the biggest spenders and have a pretty good idea about need — for instance, orthopaedic departments presumably know the number of patients each year who are being referred for hip operations. I believe that this information should also be sought by directors of public health at health authority level and that hospitals and health authorities should be combining forces to try to produce accurate figures. These could be aggregated around the country, unmet need demonstrated, and this evidence put to the Treasury as part of the argument for increased funding.

Another crucial issue is the state of the capital stock (and equipment) within the service. Each hospital and district should know the state of its capital stock and be able to produce an estimate for the cost of bringing it up to standard. This information should also be aggregated around the country and put to the Treasury as further evidence.

The United States system is demand led rather than need led. Doctors must be involved in measuring need and then must do much more work on demonstrating the effectiveness of treatment. This will need priority in clinical research and should be assisted through properly conducted medical audit with peer review. I am not keen on clinical directorates if the clinical director is to believe that he or she is in managerial command and am happier with the divisional systems with somebody at the head in whom the local consultants have confidence. I accept, however, that if clinical

109

directors are selected so that consultants have confidence in them, and if they see themselves as trying to manage through consensus, they could be a useful touchstone for managers.

Funding

I am quite keen on the concept of a designated health tax, but I understand the Treasury's reservations. I'm also interested in the concept of topping up health funds through local taxation, but I believe that the concept of a national and nationally funded health service is crucial and local taxation is basically against this. I suspect that the Treasury would, in any case, just reduce the central funding in proportion to the amount that was being raised locally.

Prioritisation

Priorities really should be decided by doctors because they consider the medical aspects first then the cost; I suspect that managers start with the costs and then try to fit in the medicine. It is difficult to give any sweeping guidance because no two patients or specialties are alike.

The basis of medicine is looking after the individual patient, so a doctor has always to base criteria for treatment on the individual not the condition. Abe Goldberg said: "it might be rare but if you've got it, it's 100%."

I am opposed to the concept of a core service because once you start thinking that way you begin to erode the whole principle of the National Health Service. I am less resistant to the concept of charging for certain hotel services but still against it because first it is the television, then it is the meal, then where next?

Purchaser-provider concept

I am opposed to the purchaser-provider concept as implemented in the government's "reforms" but would split strategic management at board or health authority level from operational management at hospital or unit level. In fact the strategic or operational split was first suggested by Griffiths,[1] but district general managers resisted it by refusing to devolve management authority.

A great deal of information will still be required on needs and unmet needs. The health board could then say to its operational

110

managers that it requires certain types of treatment from them but do this without all the bureaucracy of contracts. The health board (health authority) must have a strategic view and the power to close down units which are not needed or to open up units which are needed, if necessary. I believe that the structure being established by the government will be slow, long winded, and could allow a fudge between the purchaser and the provider; there will have to be good links between the purchaser and the provider because in order to know what to buy the purchaser will have to know what is available.

Self governing trusts

Glasgow now has an integrated health service but as soon as a single hospital opts out the integration will be lost. I strongly believe that an internal market with self governing trusts will reduce patient choice; will be bureaucratic because of the complexities of contracts, billing, and charging; and will erode the fundamental principles of the NHS. As an alternative I would really devolve management (and authority) to units; these would still be funded through the health authority but there would be no contracts — that is, hospitals would be run by managers not by health boards or health authorities.

Fundholding

In relation to fundholding practices, I'm sure that the idea of priorities being determined by thousands of individual practices is a complete nonsense. It can work only if some practices are fundholding and some are not, which inevitably means a two tier service.

I can see the comparative advantages of fundholders purchasing through family health services authorities or district health authorities using them as an agency, but I am not enthusiastic. Just because the government has come up with a daft idea, there is no need to respond with another daft idea — that is, it would be better to resist fundholding altogether.

Accountability

Direct election

I am not keen on directly elected health boards or health authorities. I have doubts about the potential calibre of those who might be elected; about how many would vote in yet another set of local elections; about possible competition either with elected members of local authorities or MPs — particularly if members were elected to represent specific areas; and about the possibility of competition between those favouring different groups of patients — for example, heart transplant candidates against mental handicap candidates.

I believe, from local council and local authority contacts, that local authorities do not want to take on health, so members of authority boards should be appointed. They must, however, come from the appropriate community; they should reflect the political and social structure of that community and they should, in some way, be representative. It must be possible to agree some criteria between the political parties, both for members (non-executive directors) and chairmen. Ultimately, however, I think that local authorities should be the strategic authority, and this will be possible in Scotland under a devolved Scottish parliament with unitary authorities.

The appointments would be advertised and selection would, as far as possible, be open, but all those interested would have to apply. I would increase the current number from five to ten and would remove health authority officials (the current executive directors) from being an integral part of the board.

Private hospitals

Private hospitals must be made more accountable for the work they do, both as a matter of broad principle and because more patients may be treated in the private sector, although their treatment will be paid for by the NHS. Private hospitals should also be more open about their staff and the hours that they work. It will be increasingly important to monitor what consultants are doing in the private sector as the sector expands to check that they are not falling down on their NHS work as a result.

Central accountability

I am ambivalent about the NHS Management Executive becoming more autonomous from ministers and the Department of Health because of loss of accountability. If current trends continue the health service could well become an agency. Politicians should not be involved in the day to day management but should concern themselves with safeguarding the fundamental principles of the NHS.

112

Community care

I broadly agree with the principles of the second Griffiths report[2] — funding is the real concern and the Labour Party is committed to ringfencing funding for community care. The area between health and social services remains grey, however, and it will be important to demarcate the various responsibilities clearly before 1993. Giving health to unitary local authorities would solve the problem.

There should be both social services and health inspectorates which are clearly independent (unlike the current social services inspectorate run as an offshoot of social services departments). These could perhaps be set up by the Audit Commission, so that they are quite independent of both health boards and health authorities and councils. They should be more than just inspectorates; they should be able to target funds to resolve problems and, to some extent, be able to prescribe solutions.

Teaching and research

Much medical teaching is done mainly on the basis of goodwill, and I am therefore concerned about the increasing financial pressures against teaching as a result of the internal market. I remain worried about the possible abolition of the "knock for knock" arrangements; it would be extremely difficult if hospitals started charging university medical schools for the teaching time of their medical staff.

Research is a real problem within the NHS. It is important to look at exactly what research is being done and, in this context, I welcome the fact that less animal research is now being done by doctors.

There must be concentration on general clinical research relating to the operation and delivery of care, together with its management, and this should involve patients. This would be much better than the current apparent emphasis on "rat strangling phenomenology" in some parts of the country. There should be closer liaison with the drug and medical equipment manufacturing companies — by this I mean more realistic charging arrangements, for instance, and if there have to be extra outpatient appointments for follow up purposes then the costs will have to be charged to the sponsoring companies, albeit at a fair and realistic rate.

1 NHS Management Enquiry. *Report*. London: DHSS, 1983 (Griffiths report.)
2 Griffiths R. *Community care. Agenda for action*. London: HMSO, 1988.

Ringfencing for the disadvantaged

NICHOLAS WINTERTON MP, *chairman, House of Commons Health Service Select Committee*

NHS reforms

I'm generally enthusiastic about the BMA's changing approach, although I'm aware that there is still great concern about the reforms being expressed by representatives of the profession. I'm pleased to have this informal channel of communication with the BMA; I believe that despite our differences there must be a great deal of common ground.

I very much support the new primacy of general practitioners; I believe that it is right for general practitioners to have more control over the way in which NHS resources are spent. I accept that even more will have to be done in the primary care setting in the future because of improvements in hospital treatment leading, generally, to shorter hospital stays, increased day case surgery, etc. I am concerned, however, that times of treatment are sometimes being reduced excessively — for example, I think that women having their first baby are sometimes discharged prematurely.

On the other hand, I believe that more deliveries could be done at home. Only a tiny percentage of babies in this country are born at home, whereas in Holland the figure is about 35%. This is possible only because Holland has an excellent after birth service: for eight hours a day for eight days families are provided with maternity aides who look after the house and children.

Community care

I can see the benefit in a resurgence of the local community hospital or general practitioner maternity unit concept. I'm generally worried, however, about the workload of general practitioners, particularly in relation to the increasing numbers of elderly people in the community and the way in which residential or nursing homes can quite suddenly be established within practices.

I'm also worried that the "NHS is coming out of care." Care of the mentally handicapped, the elderly, and, to some extent, the mentally ill is likely to come increasingly under local authority control under the new arrangements, and I'm concerned about the lack of medical input. There must be better resourcing for care in the community with ringfenced funds (I believe, incidentally, that the current specific grant for mental health is inadequate). Ringfencing or earmarked funding is crucial for care in the community because the disadvantaged have minimal voting power.

The hospital service

I'm an enthusiast for the resource management initiative and for clinical directorates. I think that the whole exercise was hijacked by the implementation of the reforms but should still be promoted strongly. Nevertheless, I'm very concerned about the information technology costs entailed in establishing the resource management initiative — perhaps £5m per hospital — but the appropriate information technology must be available to enable accurate costings and accountability.

My concern about self governing hospitals is that they might, because of competition, go for "glamour" treatments — that is, those which raise most money — which could lead to duplication of facilities, as happens in the United States. I believe that there must be a planning role at the district health authority (or possibly the regional health authority) to try to ensure that this is minimised. I strongly believe that family health services authorities and district health authorities should be merged, but I'm not really sure precisely what they should do, although the purchasing role and the responsibilities of the family health services authorities are not incompatible.

Accountability

I can see little good in an "arm's length" model of management which would treat the NHS like a corporation. I believe that there must be central political accountability to the secretary of state, although day to day management issues should be devolved down

the line. I'm generally happy with local accountability. I think that
the old health authorities were too political and that the current
non-executive directors know their stuff and are committed to the
communities they are serving.

A call for continued pressure on funding

RENEE SHORT, *former chairman, House of Commons Social Services Select Committee*

Personal priorities

Community care

I am concerned about care in the community. It needs a great deal more money, preferably new funds rather than money diverted from the acute sector. It is not sensible in terms of cost effectiveness or patient care for mentally handicapped patients, for instance, to be admitted from the community into expensive acute beds which they then block. It must be more sensible to have appropriate facilities within the community for minor medical problems and convalescence.

I accept that community care is expensive, but I'm convinced that if it is properly organised it can be cheaper — that is, more cost effective — than hospital care. I do not want to "rob Peter to pay Paul"; I think that the BMA should be campaigning for new money for community care.

Booking systems

The NHS must sort out its outpatient booking systems. There really must be proper appointments rather than block bookings for a half day. I'm sure that many patients believe that going to outpatient departments is a complete waste of time and this, therefore, is a key factor in non-attendance rates.

Day surgery

I believe there must be better use of surgeons and surgical beds throughout the service. In particular there should be a further increase in the amount of day surgery, which would lead to less bed

117

blocking and reduced waiting lists; it might also make surgeons' jobs more interesting.

This is a matter for the profession to sort out. I'm not sure that performance related pay would be appropriate because of the potential unfairness in relation to the different types of case mixes in different types of hospital.

Research

I believe that the medical profession often unfairly gets the blame for what are really management problems; doctors must have the clinical space to innovate and develop treatments and procedures. Somehow management has to recognise and support the work doctors do in pushing back the frontiers of medical science.

I have been a member of the Medical Research Council, whose work is of the very highest quality, higher, I believe, than some work done solely in the NHS. Research is expensive but it must be supported. Those working with Michael Peckham, the new NHS director of research and development, should be prepared to use the same type of approach as the MRC — that is, inadequate proposals should be turned down, ongoing work should be carefully monitored, and, if the standards are low or the research is getting nowhere, the funding should be stopped.

Purchaser-provider concept

Hospitals must know what is going on in their local community. They must be able to respond to local need and be flexible in the services they provide. They cannot afford to isolate themselves, as self governing trusts might do; they have to be in touch with the local population and the local authority.

Contact within local authorities is pretty poor now, particularly between the medical profession and the social services departments; but with self governing trusts it could become even worse. I'm sure that trusts must be brought back into health authority control to ensure they are responsive to need and not just to financial considerations.

I believe that the purchaser-provider split is entirely commercial and that the Labour party has not yet really decided its position. What is needed is for heads to be banged together where necessary, targets set rather more carefully and the huge diversion of commercial contracts divorced from actual need should be discontinued.

Funding

If the Treasury is to move on health care funding strong positive arguments must be put up. I am keen to see continued intense pressure from the BMA on funding. There must be more money available through the shift from defence spending alone.

I do not accept the "bottomless pit" argument. We need arguments for money targeted for specific areas, not only to go towards the Department of Health but also, for instance, to the Department of Education, to ensure adequate funding for medical education.

I'm sure that funding for health care is best raised through general taxation; I certainly have doubts about raising much money through local taxation, which is a highly political issue at present. We must press the government for a funding system that can be seen to address unmet need more satisfactorily.

Accountability

I accept that many members of the old health authorities were appointed mainly on party lines and this was not satisfactory. I'm not happy, however, with non-executive directors coming almost exclusively from commerce and industry. I believe that members of authorities should include doctors (both providers and purchasers), university representatives where appropriate (perhaps appointees from polytechnics or colleges of further education in non-teaching districts), a community health council representative, and a local authority representative. With all these, however, the health authority should try to find the right individuals and approach them first so that the balance of the board can be maintained — that is, rather than asking the various organisations to nominate or elect individuals of their own choice.

Public action

Members of the public are full of goodwill towards those who provide care at all levels. We should take them into our confidence, explain our difficulties and how they affect patient care, and so encourage them to put pressure on ministers and their own parliamentary representatives, who *do* listen on the whole.

A regional approach to health

GREG PARSTON, *executive director, Office for Public Management*

Funding

Increasing effectiveness

I do not believe in the "bottomless pit" argument; I think that levels of need and demand will eventually be able to be assessed and that the purchaser-provider concept may help this process. I'm quite sure that the funding of the NHS is low by any international comparison; this is because we pay our staff less, we put less finance to capital, and centralised control has enabled tight rationing of resources.

We probably need to increase the proportion of gross domestic product spent on health by 2%. We must also, however, increase effectiveness through audit and make better use of the finance we already have. The number of outpatient clinics could be increased together with day case surgery — Cambridge (which is comparatively progressive) has a rate of outpatient surgery of 15% whereas in some parts of Arizona it reaches 50%. In addition, more effort could be put into reducing the length of bed stay. In one part of the United States they have been able to reduce bed stay from 800 to 250 bed days/1000 population/year; in the United Kingdom our figure tends to be over 1000 bed days/1000 population/year.

Raising finance

The current general taxation system guarantees access of health care to all; any other system would have to do the same. The Canadian system is quite good, but there is still a clear two tier service with those who can afford it "topping up." Priority in relation to any health care system must be towards the poor and deprived in society who cannot "top up."

I have looked into the possibility of raising money through local taxation but believe this might best be done through regional rather than through local government. The Scotland, Wales, and Northern Ireland models work quite well and the region will probably have much more influence under the purchaser-provider arrangement. Local government already has the ability to raise money for certain services, but, albeit against the tide running in most of Europe, this government is unwilling to give local government more power but might be prepared to consider a regional approach to health. We would certainly need to consider the question of regional accountability and election or appointment of members if money was to be raised by the region.

Allocation

I thought that the Resource Allocation Working Party (RAWP) approach was sensible until the formula was changed to allow money to be taken away, particularly from the Thames regions. The original targets were to be achieved incrementally, and if the process had been allowed to proceed without interference the upheaval in London might have been much less dramatic. Allocation through weighted capitation will result again in money being taken away from some regions.

Prioritisation

It is difficult to have public debate on prioritisation at national level, but district health authorities do have the responsibility to consult with the public before making priorities. I'm not certain about the full value of the Oregon approach except that it does at least seem to make the debate on prioritisation explicit. Again the arguments should not just be about rationing but about making the service, and particularly treatment, more effective — there is a great deal to do on making treatment more effective.

Central accountability

I support the "next steps" approach and believe that much progress has already been made towards this; for instance, the pace of negotiations during the ambulance drivers' dispute led to the development of a clearer direct line relationship between the secretary of state and the chief executive, Duncan Nichol, without the intermediary role of civil servants. I believe that the permanent secretary and his civil servants should not be in the direct line of management down to the NHS Management Executive but should deal with policy advice rather than operational matters. I'm concerned about the management executive's move to Leeds as the chief executive will have to stay in London most of the time, as will other members of the executive, which will disrupt its work.

Local accountability

Non-executive directors of health authorities should be seen to be rooted in the local population. There should be less centralisation in their appointment, although I would expect that the region or centre should continue to have right to veto. Appointments should be made, however, only after local discussion and serious analysis of the contributions that different individuals could make. The key role of non-executive directors is to move the organisation forward in a strategic sense by acting as guardians of the authorities' overall objectives for health and health care.

I believe that regional health authorities will become the "branch offices" of the NHS Management Executive. In which case, and if they are not responsible for raising a regional health rate, there may be less need for a regional board including non-executive directors in future.

I suspect that there will be a move to reduce the number of regions, perhaps even to a half of the current number. There may need to be only one or two regional health authorities covering London; there is not enough managerial or public health talent around to service the current number of regions properly in their new regulatory role, and, if regional health authorities do become branch offices, the executive will probably want fewer of them to decrease the lines of accountability.

I accept that trusts will probably come to report to regional health authorities and that reducing the number of regional health authorities will lead to many trusts being accountable to each. I believe, however, that the regional health authority will have a limited role in relation to trusts, which will mainly be to do with quality and accreditation. District health authorities are already arguing that they cannot easily put quality standards in contracts, and at the same time the good trusts are arguing that somebody needs to keep the "cowboys" down. I'm sure that the principal role of the region in relation to trusts will be to accredit and check that corners are not being cut in relation to quality.

Purchaser-provider concept

District health authorities as purchasers

I was against the purchaser-provider system to start off with, but I have been convinced of its worth by what I believe is the unintended responsibility that has been left for district health authorities as principal purchasers to assure the health of the population. I'm happy with the concept of district health authorities as prime purchasers and "health assurance agencies."

To ensure that this role is given proper priority it will be necessary for directly managed units to be put very much at arm's length. District health authorities and district general managers really cannot continue to see themselves principally as providers when they should be concentrating on needs assessment, planning, and achieving health targets.

Nevertheless, I'm not sure that all directly managed units can just become self governing trusts. This is a difficult area. I suggest that directly managed units might have their own boards and could be on contract to district health authorities, although there would still be the difficulty of line managerial accountability to the district general manager. This would not be satisfactory as hospital and community unit politics could easily dominate more purchaser related issues.

Competition

I do not believe the managerial talent is ready, nor is there the support to run many more trusts at present; the current 57 are the high fliers. It is crucial that the regional health authority seeks to regulate and ensure competition even between acute units and community units, both of which might, for instance, seek to run outpatient surgical clinics and extended home care. I can see that self governing hospitals might try to stop this type of competition by taking over the profitable parts of community units. The government could also legislate to make it impossible for self governing trusts to be "profitable" by making them "public benefit corporations."

Fundholding

General practitioner fundholding can work if the fundholders are on subcontract to the district health authority as the prime purchaser. The district health authority has a statutory responsibility for the health of its population; fundholders have no such responsibility, so therefore the district health authority should have the power to require certain outcomes from fundholders in relation to quality and health targets. The regional health authority could try to hold fundholders to specific quality criteria, but district health authorities might be better suited to this as the number of fundholders increases. I'm sure that district health authorities and family health services authorities will eventually amalgamate and that fundholders will purchase through consortia or agencies (for example, the district health authority) to maintain their purchasing power.

Community care

I'm convinced that the social services should take the lead on community care, although they are even more stretched financially and generally have more managerial problems than health authorities — for example, the social services are currently lagging well behind in relation to the purchaser-provider split compared with health authorities.

The new money coming to local authorities from the social security budget must be ringfenced. I accept that funding of community care through local authorities could be a real problem but believe it is nevertheless worth trying the model, which is sensible in theory. I accept that the health authority *could* take over social services if it could get rid of the provider role, which currently preoccupies management. The Northern Ireland health and social services boards seem to work well, but what role would be left for local government and how would health authorities be held accountable to the community?

Soft approaches and changing roles

PAMELA CHARLWOOD, *director, and* STEPHEN HALPERN, *project development manager, Institute of Health Services Management*

Funding

We strongly believe that the NHS continues to be underfunded on the basis of international comparisons and that the public debate should be brought back to the question of funding after the diversion of the reforms. After the strong arguments for better funding put forward in the three collaborative Institute of Health Services Management, Royal College of Nursing, and BMA documents the institute produced a further document in 1988 on alternative delivery and funding of the health services.[1] This study tested different options for funding and delivery against the criteria on which the NHS was established — namely, equity, comprehensiveness, and equality of access. The institute is now doing detailed work on updating this document with a view to publishing a new version in the autumn. Alternatives to general taxation that will be considered include a system of social insurance plus top ups, the problem with this being how to maintain the fundamental criteria while increasing funding.

We believe that raising more money for health through local taxation would be difficult, firstly, because it would probably have to come through the local authority — under the current system at least — and, secondly, it could lead to inequity of provision in different geographical areas. Nevertheless, the concept of a health authority being able to levy a local health rate (equivalent, for instance, to water rates) could be explored.

The introduction of the weighted capitation method of allocating funding is one of the most significant reforms. If it happened overnight it would be disastrous for London, but it is not in fact to be filtered down from regional health authorities until 1993-4 or

125

later. Delaying the introduction will cushion the London teaching hospitals, but we would prefer a more purposeful move to the new system sooner rather than later. In theory, weighted capitation is the first stage of money following the patient; in reality, money will be following the contract at health authority level.

Purchaser-provider concept

Generally we accept that the purchaser-provider system is here to stay and welcome this, but we cannot see purchasing and providing continuing in district health authorities. Family health services authorities and district health authorities are likely to merge and we think that purchasing should be separated from providing. There is a developing management consensus that district health authorities should purchase and that all provider units (not just self governing trusts) should be moved to "arm's length."

The main problems with fundholding are the negative effect on the doctor-patient relationship that could occur through cash limiting and how to plan a coordinated service for the local population. General practitioner fundholders are responding to need in the surgery, but how can the needs and demands of the population as a whole be catered for? Nevertheless, some fundholders have been able to break through the various bureaucratic channels and systems in the service and have been making deals with real benefits for their patients. We acknowledge the point made by Ray Robinson of the King's Fund that fundholders have also been able to secure some changes in hospital clinical practice when they have been able to make deals directly with consultants or clinical directors.

Local accountability

We perceive a real problem with many of the current non-executive directors of district health authorities. The white paper, *Working for Patients*,[2] almost excluded anyone with a direct health interest, but we must have informed, interested people capable of doing the job. Many of the present cadre are experts in finance or commerce but untutored in relation to health need.

We cannot see a change in the "political" appointment of health authority chairmen, but we do need better advice on selecting non-executive directors. Some district health authorities went through a detailed selection process to try to pick informed people from a range of backgrounds but many did not.

We're not keen on the direct election of health authority members; again we may get entirely the wrong sort of people and this would also risk making health care a party political football locally as well as nationally.

We're dubious about the capacity of community health councils to be effective with their current level of resources. We accept that health authorities will need to take evidence from a very wide range of interests when planning or purchasing care for the local population. We should probably incorporate consumer representation formally into the purchaser system to encourage checks on quality from the patient's point of view. In addition, we accept that there should not be a total barrier between the purchaser and the provider in relation to medical advice.

Central accountability

We believe strongly that there should be organisational distance between the secretary of state and the chief executive, Duncan Nichol. More executive power should be given to the NHS Management Executive, but we're greatly concerned about its imminent move to Leeds, particularly as some of the key players will continue to be based in London. We cannot see the need for such a large number of civil servants to be involved in the Department of Health and would support the concept of the department being turned into a "next steps" type of agency with a small number of civil servants concerned only in policy issues.

Regional health authorities are "muscling up" at present, but we're concerned about their accountability. Are they to be the local arms of the management executive? Will the management executive eventually devolve accountability of self governing trusts to the region?

Medical audit and effectiveness of treatment

Work on medical audit and effectiveness of treatment should be led by doctors, but we believe there is a need for management input and support. We can accept a layered approach to audit with work on pure techniques and outcomes of specific treatments left largely to doctors, through the wider participation of health professionals in clinical audit, to the involvement of professionals and managers when quality parameters are injected into contracts.

Integration of primary and secondary care

We can see the benefit of single large district general hospitals providing a core service for the community with local, smaller community hospitals for outpatient clinics, day cases, day care, and convalescence, perhaps without resident medical staff but covered by local general practitioners. We're interested in the concept of polyclinics, with a variety of health professionals working together, and would raise the concept of salaried general practitioners in this context. Such clinics might be well suited to inner city areas and, if suitably resourced, could deal with the "walking wounded" (people presenting at accident and emergency departments for primary care) during opening hours.

Community care

We are extremely concerned about the false boundaries between health and social care. Both local authorities and health authorities are involved in community work. Contrary to the model of local authorities "commissioning" health care, health and welfare authorities could cover health and community care.

1 Institute of Health Services Management. *Working party on alternative delivery and funding of health services.* London: IHSM, 1988.
2 Secretaries of State for Health, Wales, Northern Ireland and Scotland. *Working for patients.* London: HMSO, 1989. (Cmnd 555.)

The increasing power of the consumer

BRIAN EDWARDS, *regional general manager, Trent Regional Health Authority*

Planning

With the reforms there is now a different approach to planning, which seeks to gain outcomes for a community. Therefore, whereas in the past it was the providers that needed planning now it is the purchasers. Nevertheless, the providers still need to be accountable for their performance and I see the region fulfilling this role.

I also believe that the region will have to take on the role of market regulator and developer. In the United States recently there has been a notable increase in "vertical integration," where purchasers have been getting too cosy with some providers; this can frustrate the market and is not always in the best interests of consumers, so it needs close monitoring.

A key priority for planning will be the implementation of *The Health of the Nation*.[1] I believe that it can be done through general practitioner contracts (with incentives) and district health authority contracts. However, I think that most of the levers are located around primary care and we are currently searching for the limited number of "golden levers" which will lead to the most significant health gain.

Assessment of need

We must have better assessment of need, and this may eventually enable a stronger case to be argued with the Treasury for better investment in the service. In particular what is required (a challenge for the BMA) would be the production of a series of treatment and care indices, which would give a good return on investment; I recognise that the Treasury is not likely to respond immediately, but such indices would become more valuable over a period of time if they were shown to be credible.

Funding

Is insurance such a bad thing? I believe strongly in our present NHS, but an entirely free health service for all will increasingly be beyond our capacity. Demographic change and technological advance will lead to an increasing gap between expectation and what can be provided and third parties will be happy to exploit this; I'm not advocating private insurance for all but I believe that we can accommodate more insurance alongside many of the values we have within the NHS. A ratio of 80% NHS to 20% insured funding would be acceptable and the insurance input could be used more effectively to benefit the service; providers could extend their non-NHS income by offering, for instance, routine screening. This would give patients more choice and would also bring more income into the service The formidable ethical challenges this would present would be worth wrestling with.

I have considered the concept of hotel charges, but I'm not very keen as it could be the start of a slide down a slippery slope. There could be more incentives for people to insure for primary care or for insurance schemes through employment; I am aware, however, that too great a swing towards the private sector could destabilise the NHS. I'm intrigued by the concept of a local health tax or health rate, preferably controlled by the health authority — this is worth exploring.

As well as seeking more money to fund health from the population we must also be seen to be making the health service more efficient.

Primary and secondary care

Consultants' role

I support the shift of health care to the primary care environment wherever this is cost effective and the shift on the centre of gravity of the NHS this implies. There continues to be a key role for consultants, who must be involved in management. The profession must allow the emergence of "leaders," who will be senior consultants but not always clinical directors. These consultants, who must have the confidence of their colleagues, are the ones who should be appointed to hospital boards. There should also be a consultant of

130

this type on health authority (purchaser) boards. I'm convinced that hospital medicine needs to be connected into the purchasing role somehow (together with general practitioners), but I prefer there to be one consultant and one general practitioner on a health authority board than a small medical advisory group.

District general hospitals

I believe that there will need to be significant changes in the pattern of district general hospital stock over the next few years, and thus there will be fewer beds in total. I have doubts whether there is the political or the professional will to undertake this rationalisation, but there should be fewer, perhaps larger, district general hospitals with a real core service. The practical approach would be to develop a vision of the shape of the hospital service towards the turn of the century and aim to move towards that by targeting development on the key sites. At the same there would need to be development or bolstering up of smaller time community units and hospitals.

Integration

I am keen on the integration of primary and secondary care and particularly the concept of shared care. In diabetes, for instance, general practitioners can provide a small amount of the care exclusively and the hospital service likewise, but most should be shared care, which might even be contributed to by occupational health services. I accept that the purchaser-provider concept could make this difficult to develop but believe that purchasers have the power to insist on being able to purchase shared care packages.

Consumerism

I think that consumers themselves will begin to demand such an integrated approach, for instance in relation to maternity care: "birth plans" are already being prepared in some areas. We must recognise that consumers will have increasing power, will be increasingly discriminating and less grateful for their care, and will be demanding more choices. Only comparatively small numbers need to take an active approach to the market to frustrate attempts at planning. Consumerism will be fuelled by the citizen's and patient's charters.

I am a strong supporter of the general practitioner's gatekeeper role but believe that this could come under real threat, at least in

131

part because the patients themselves may seek to bypass general practitioners and go directly to specialists. In addition, I believe that it will not be long before provider units are tempted to appeal directly to patients to walk in off the street. In the past the gatekeeper role has been reinforced largely through the NHS culture and through tradition, but in future there may need to be more use of financial mechanisms to secure it. Obviously if patients are paying with their own money then they should have the choice.

Although I would like it not to be so, I believe that health care reacts to financial levers as much as any other system. The use of those levers must be monitored extremely carefully or they could come totally to dominate the service, as in the "rubber windmill" exercise in East Anglia.

Universities and medical schools

I am concerned about medical schools, which are being squeezed in almost every way at present. The universities are being squeezed through the Universities Funding Council, the teaching hospitals are being squeezed through the purchaser-provider concept and the service increment for teaching and research (SIFTR), and there is also pressure on research funding, the structure of which is changing rapidly.

There are probably too many medical schools, although they might be producing roughly the right number of graduates. We probably do not need more doctors but we do need to review their roles in relation to other health professionals.

1 Secretary of State for Health. *The health of the nation*. London: HMSO, 1991. (Cm 1523.)

Purchasing primary care

MICHAEL O'BRIEN, *director of public health, East Anglia Regional Health Authority*

Assessment of need

Proper assessment of need is crucial but, in view of the current fluidity at district level (that is, potential mergers of district health authorities and family health services authorities) some of this might best be done by the region. I believe that assessment of need for care *should* be done at district level but that districts are currently really assessing only secondary care needs.

I am concerned about local authorities assessing need for some aspects of community care and acting as "commissioners of health care." My experience is that local politicians are often ill informed on technical issues and lack the willingness to be informed but, despite this, are very willing to interfere on the basis of belief.

I'm also concerned at the quoted proposition by one general practitioner that "general practitioners can assess need intuitively." The practice population is much too small and too mobile to act as a sensible epidemiological base. Work on referrals from general practice showed that most conditions which are comparatively common in hospital work are rare in individual practices — the work apparently showed a fourfold variation from one year to the next, making the likelihood of many conditions appearing almost completely random.

Model for provision

I think that it will be very difficult to dole out finance sensibly unless there is a significant population (more than 250 000) on which to base assessment of need. I'm concerned that the NHS reforms have given district health authorities and family health services

133

authorities the wrong roles. District health authorities measure need and purchase care. In fact they purchase only secondary care. As the vast majority of needs are met in the primary care sector district health authorities (or the regional health authority) should buy primary care — that is, fund general practitioners or consortia of general practitioners on the basis of population and need. That would leave family health services authorities to buy secondary care, acting as agents for general practitioners.

Family health services authorities would identify with general practitioners and liaise with them to agree aggregate needs. The family health services authority, suitably funded, would then arrange contracts with and payments to local provider units on behalf of general practitioners.

I am confident that most family health services authorities see themselves as purchasers. Some, however, see themselves as providers — that is, as line managers for general practitioners.

Role of region

In smaller regions it is comparatively easy to know all that is going on. Thus it is not difficult for the regional health authority to pass down funds on the basis of population and assessed need. In larger regions it is less easy to know comprehensively all that goes on. It may be, therefore, that in these regions something smaller than the regional health authority but larger than the district will emerge either through amalgamation of districts or splitting up of the region — these divisions used to be known as areas.

Hospital management

I believe that there is a future for resource management and clinical directorates. I know from experience that this type of peer pressure can actually lead to change in and to more cost effective clinical practice. It also has the bonus of putting consultants in the driving seat.

I see two significant changes coming by the turn of the century. Firstly, the distinction between general practitioners and consultants may become more blurred, with consultants consulting in the community and general practitioners doing more specialist work. Concerns are being raised about the standards of surgical practice among those general practitioners doing minor surgery (for example, instances of not fully excising skin cancers), but if general practitioners are encouraged to do their sessions in hospitals they could come within the hospital audit procedures, which could only be beneficial.

Secondly, it is quite likely that more hospital specialist care will be provided by non-medical scientists over the next few years — for example, specialists in molecular biology and genetics. The whole role of doctors compared with other health professionals is likely to change.

Accountability

Doctors are accountable to individual patients; to the profession (through the General Medical Council, the royal colleges, etc); and for the resources they use. The employing authority should share that accountability both up to government and down to its population, but, in relation to the population, the situation is currently unsatisfactory.

I believe that accountability at general practitioner level is probably satisfactory because practitioners are so close to the patient. There is a particular need for better accountability at provider unit level. Perhaps each provider unit should have some form of watchdog group as part of its total quality management arrangements.

Funding

We need the stability of most health funding being through central government — that is, the Treasury. Good health is in the national interest and it should be a national payment. I'm doubtful about ability to raise extra money locally because, if done through local authorities, it will be highly political, and if done through voluntary contributions it will be sporadic with no guaranteed level of income. A voluntary approach works well when it is for high tech equipment such as dialysis machines and scanners but tends to be much less successful in relation to extra facilities for the disabled and mentally handicapped, for instance.

135

District health authorities and need for credibility with consultants

JACK HOWELL, *chairman, Southampton and South West Hampshire District Health Authority*

Need to define the problem

In approaching health policy, it is essential to define the question before attempting to define the solution. The 1974 and 1982 reorganisations offered solutions to undefined questions and, before the 1982 reorganisation had time to work, along came the Griffiths management inquiry. The Griffiths recommendations[1] were incomplete in that, in relation to medical involvement in management, they did not give a strong enough lead towards the concept of clinical directorates.

At the same time the service began to suffer a financial squeeze. It had been used to receiving 3-4% per annum growth money in real terms and this was cut to 1% per annum. There had been obvious waste, inefficiency, and lack of direction, and the reduction in funding might have been expected to lead to an increase in efficiency. To some extent it did, but there were also a number of politically damaging crises in the service, culminating in the heart surgery problem at the children's hospital in Birmingham and the strong line taken by three of the royal college presidents.

Role of doctors in the hospital service

One of the problems before the reforms was the lack of involvement of consultants in managing the service generally, although they were extremely influential in the spending of NHS resources, particularly in the acute sector — at least until services such as those for mentally handicapped patients and the care of elderly people became designated as priority services.

Managers were appointed but were weak in the face of the

136

influence of consultants and there was little opportunity to plan or counterbalance the activities of the consultants in the acute sector. I'm not critical of the consultants themselves — I accept that most were arguing in the interests of their patients and that this model actually served the NHS quite well over the past 20 years in providing generally good quality secondary care very cheaply.

Nevertheless, it was perceived that the structure was not necessarily designed to meet the needs of the community; one of the aims of the most recent reforms has been to change that balance. This has inevitably led to the loss of power for senior hospital doctors. In essence I believe that the previous structure did not have the confidence of the government but that if the profession had addressed the question of financial accountability earlier things might have been different. I support the resource management initiative and clinical directorates, but these came too late.

Purchaser-provider concept

District health authorities

There was little planned purchasing before the reforms, although health authorities, in handing down funds to units, were purchasing, though not in an explicit manner. The benefit of the new arrangements for a health authority is that requirements can be specified — that is, you know what you expect for your money, and you know if you do not get it. Consultants in provider units cannot now determine where additional money will be allocated but, once allocated, they *must* be involved in determining how it is used.

A particular problem for consultants in many authorities is that there is only one doctor on the district health authority's management board, and this is usually a director of public health. It is crucial, when the district health authority is allocating specific funds or purchasing, that it has credibility with senior hospital doctors. I think it extremely important to have an active medical advisory committee to the health authority and I would propose the Southampton model for discussion. The advisory committee has as members nine consultants and three general practitioners. These are chosen (that is, rather than being elected), with a view to their having the confidence of the profession and the district health authority. The committee meets mainly with the executive directors but, occasionally, with the whole authority.

In relation to access by the local community into the decision making process, the chairman of the community health council is invited to attend health authority meetings, including the confidential part. I accept the need for accountability to the community.   It is extremely important for the profession to work with managers and people like non-executive board members. We must get across to these people and the public the potential professional conflict for doctors between their accountability to individual patients and their accountability to use resources cost effectively. Doctors need to *show* that they are using resources effectively, and the challenge is to prevent the government being able to say that doctors and others waste health money.

Self governing trusts

In relation to self governing trusts I have prefered the concept of "arm's length" directly managed units, but we must wait and see. I wonder how much control a health authority as a purchaser will actually have over self governing hospitals — that is, will it be able to stop them closing down some services and increasing others because there is a better market for them, perhaps from other purchasers?

Fundholding

On fundholding practices again I want to wait and see, but I'm concerned that if there is a great increase in fundholders it will reduce the health authority's power to plan for its local population.

Conclusion

In general I would like the profession to be more positive about the new health service and to join the managers in trying to make it work for patients. Managers should learn about the doctors' professional ethic, but doctors should also try to understand the role of managers.

1 NHS Management Enquiry. *Report*. London: DHSS, 1983. (Griffiths report.)

Self governing trust: a stable first year

MAURICE BURROWS, *former chairman, Wirral Health Authority, and chairman, Wirral Hospital Trust*

Purchaser-provider concept

The district health authority used to be totally dominated by the hospitals in the area and had no time to concentrate on the "public health." Therefore, splitting purchasers from providers was a good thing. I believe, incidentally, that combining the district health authority and family health services authority would also be beneficial.

The self governing trust has been more forward thinking on health needs than the district health authority so far. As yet the trust has been given no steer on district health authority priorities. Waiting list problems, however, now belong to the district health authority, which must assess the need, seeking help to do this from general practitioners and the community health council. I believe the reason that the trust has been ahead of the district health authority is probably because of the energy and drive of the people managing the trust. The district health authority is now beginning to pay regard to the "public health," and this is encouraging.

Lobbying by self governing trusts

The self governing trust has been doing its own work to build expectation and to lobby the local population (including the community health council and voluntary agencies) on what should be provided. This sort of approach will be important for trusts as Mersey region, for instance, now has only two purchasing consortia covering all the purchasing districts in the region. This will mean that they will be somewhat distant from and less informed about their local popultations; such a system will put a trust that has done its research into a strong position.

139

Feedback

I can see the benefit of feedback medical advice from provider doctors back to the purchasing authority, but Wirral district health authority has not done this. It is using general practitioners only for advice and is receiving provider advice only through informal channels. There are, however, meetings between the district health authority and self governing trust boards, together with informal discussion between the chief executives. Wirral Hospital Trust is unique among the first wave trusts in having two consultants (clinical directors) — a physician and a psychiatrist — as executive directors on the board. The hospital council manages the hospital and is composed of clinical directors who are appointed, not elected, but do have the confidence of their clinical colleagues. They control about 73% of hospital expenditure.

Fundholding

There have been no fundholders in the Wirral area in the first year, so there has been stability. I'm slightly concerned about fundholding as some general practitioners can be mavericks and could be destabilising. It would be more sensible if fundholders were to join in consortia to talk about their needs and present them to the district health authority. The self governing trust is talking directly to general practitioners, and the district health authority should also be sharing its ideas for future strategy with fundholders, so that a consensus can be achieved for long term planning. Indeed, there should be a forum for fundholders and non-fundholders to join together to promote rational planning.

It is the district health authority's duty to set priorities and give a direction to health care in the district. My concern about fundholders is that their emphasis in individual group practices may not reflect the general thrust of the district. There can be ways of dealing with this issue, but it needs to be recognised.

Directly managed units

Directly managed units do not fit in very easily with the purchaser-provider concept. There is pressure on district health authority managers to ensure that their directly managed units do not fold, so they could be more partial towards them than they are to self governing trusts, for which they are not accountable. All hospitals, therefore, should become trusts or they should all be managed at arm's length to distinguish clearly the strategic and operational roles.

Accountability

Purchasing authorities must be able to assess local need and demand by using general practitioner input, community health councils, and surveys. I'm not keen on the concept of elected board members. It's better to have executive members on the board because they now share responsibility for the final decisions — that is, there is corporate responsibility. Five non-executive directors is certainly better than 18, but the board must be seen as a corporate unit of 11 in total.

I believe that the trust is accountable to the local population. It has to account through the media almost every day. It has regular meetings with the officers of the community health council and organises regular meetings with organisations which might have an interest (the League of Friends, MIND, Psoriasis Association, etc) in addition to the required annual public meeting. The trust board is a statutory body, therefore accountable directly to the secretary of state. I accept that there is a dotted management line to the region, but self governing trusts do not have a management relationship with the regional health authority, although they do meet the chairman on a regular basis.

My experience as chairman of a district health authority, with its large membership of 19, including local council nominees, leads me to much prefer the new constitution. Executive directors carry their full share of responsibility as board members and their contribution is vital, alongside that of the non-executive directors, all of whom live in the district.

I'm concerned, however, about how capital is going to be allocated in future, as this is a key controlling factor. It is currently funded through external financing limits, which have to be checked in relation to regional plans and gain purchaser approval; I know that regional health authority chairmen believe that all development should be through regions, but I'm not happy with this type of control.

HEALTH POLICY AND ECONOMICS

Roles, models, and lack of government imagination

DAVID J HUNTER, *director, Nuffield Institute for Health Services Studies*

Commissioning of health care

The Institute for Public Policy Research (IPPR) model of unitary local authorities commissioning health care[1] was a serious attempt to provide a real role for local authorities and to improve public accountability, which is lacking in the NHS. Some local authorities have an extremely good record in relation to health (for example, those involved in the healthy cities project), and *because* of their local accountability through elected members would be in good position to purchase health care. Local government is much maligned, particularly by this government, but has the infrastructure to do the job.

There has been a mixed response to the IPPR document but, interestingly, some district general managers have supported it precisely because there would be improved public accountability. The old health authorities were able to sustain an argument that they were accountable through their local authority members in particular to the local population, but this is no longer the case.

I can see the alternative case for bringing health and community care under the auspices of the health authority, but the model falls down because of the lack of accountability of health authorities at present. It would in any case be extremely difficult to do so explicitly and all in one go because there would be fierce resistance from local authorities. Moreover, health authorities might be inclined to pursue a medical rather than a social model of care, which policy over the years has sought to move away from. An institutional orientation is hard to shift.

Nevertheless, we should still tackle the question of the non-executive members of health authorities. As a non-executive director

145

myself I know the crucial role that the health authority has in purchasing health care, but I am not yet entirely sure of my own role in this area. The role of non-executive directors should be clarified; selection should be more open or at least the criteria for selection should be more open. If non-executive directors cannot claim to "represent" the community then it is crucial to ensure sampling of consumer opinion through surveys, public forums, etc. I am doubtful about the role of community health councils; they too need their membership to be reviewed if they are not to fade away completely. Health authorities as presently constituted cannot perform effectively as "champions of the people" because they lack legitimacy. Community health councils are not representative of the community either and need to be supplemented by other ways of communicating with, consulting, and empowering the public.

Community care

Although ministers are still reaffirming their commitment to their version of the proposals put forward in the second Griffiths report,[2] I think that they are doing so with less and less conviction. There must be serious questions about whether this particular government could bring itself to transfer such large sums of money, whatever they turn out to be — and the delay must be a cause for concern — from the central social security budget to local authorities. It's possible that *Caring for People*[3] will be implemented in a piecemeal manner, or only in part, or that health authorities will have to take on some of the care by default. If *Caring for People* is to be implemented as intended the money ought at least to be earmarked for social services; even if it is there will still be competing pressures between adult and child care with the likelihood that priority will be given to children because of their emotive appeal and current political and social pressures and concerns (such as the issue of child abuse).

There are two indications that the government may be lukewarm about *Caring for People*. Firstly, it has not yet decided the sum of money to be transferred to local authorities, which is making local authority planning very difficult, particularly general and community care planning. Secondly, I know of at least two Department of Health sponsored pilot schemes which could be seen as undermining the government's own proposals or at the very least calling into question its commitment to a leading role for local government. These centre on general practitioners and primary care services serving as key gateways to social care.

Planning

I see an increasing role for regional health authorities in planning a regional health strategy in relation to *The Health of the Nation*.[4] I am concerned that there may not be sufficient expertise available at district level; the region may be better placed to pool scarce skills and resources. In addition to encouraging implementation of a health strategy the region will also need to have a policing role to regulate the market. We need to be very careful about regulation, however, because of the cost and doubtful efficiency of regulation; we have witnessed, for instance, the vast cost and new industry of regulation in the United States. At district level I can perceive an increasing tension between managers and public health consultants. In fact there needs to be a symbiotic relationship rather than competition between the two. Non-medical general managers should be prepared to learn more about epidemiology and health needs if they are to take their new purchasing role seriously and be appropriately equipped.

Purchaser-provider concept

One benefit of the purchaser-provider distinction may be that planning will now become a key role for purchaser managers; before the reforms managers were generally "fire fighting" and had no real time, opportunity, or inclination for proper planning. I'm not convinced that the purchaser-provider concept relates well to what the health service is really about — a "sickness" service rather than a health service — in fact I'm not sure that it was created with any key objectives or strategy in mind. It has evolved and changed shape over time but it offers an opportunity if nurtured with care. However, is the NHS about health or sickness? Can it be about both?

I am not too concerned about general practitioner budget holders. They do not have much purchasing power at present, which is one of the reasons why they will begin to purchase through consortia. I would be happy with the model of fundholders using the family health services authority or district health authority as a purchasing agent. My greatest concern is over the concept of the self governing trust; the accountability of trusts is not at all clear but certainly it is not to the local population and the more trusts do deals with each other and fix the market, the more they could come to dominate the way in which health care is delivered rather than the purchasers. There is also the issue of accountability upwards to parliament. How is this to be resolved? Can trusts be given freedom — and if so, how much — while still being accountable to parliament as part of a *national* health service?

Central accountability

I would like to see a much greater devolution of executive management control to the NHS Management Executive. I'm not so sure about moving completely to a corporation model, but the executive should be an arm's length "next steps" agency. The number of civil servants in the Department of Health probably needs to be cut down. Is a 2:1 ratio between "policy" officials and "management" officials correct? I am concerned that there is not yet any noticeable corporate culture or identity within the NHS Management Executive and that, if the move to Leeds does not address this, the much stronger culture of the civil service in the DoH could dominate and overshadow the management executive. There is definitely a need to define the role of the NHS Management Executive more clearly so that both its members and the NHS can understand its objectives.

Funding

I'm quite sure that general taxation is the most efficient way of both collecting and distributing funds for health care. I cannot see a specifically earmarked health tax being acceptable to the Treasury, but more money could be raised for health through national insurance. The concept of raising money for health through local taxation is interesting, but the transaction costs of raising and administering the tax or health rate could be quite large.

A national social insurance scheme might well be worth considering, as is some form of long term care insurance for elderly people — an area of growing concern which is not being addressed by policy makers. There is something along these lines operating in both the United States and Germany, and this sort of money could help to fund community care and the health costs of the increasing numbers of elderly people. It would work rather like an occupational pension. Maybe employers should contribute to a scheme — Sir Roy Griffiths implied as much in his community care report.[2]

In relation to prioritisation, I believe that improved "elegant muddling through" on prioritisation practised by the medical profession and managers, together with rationing by waiting, is rather better than the complex, subjective, and spuriously objective approach being used in Oregon. I know of various projects being undertaken in the United Kingdom (for example, in mid Essex) to explore the possibilities of an Oregon type approach, but while a district may refuse to provide a service to its population I cannot believe that a district can refuse to purchase a treatment for an individual in its area under the terms of the current NHS Act, which require the secretary of state to provide a comprehensive service. Most NHS provision is in any case not of a fanciful or cosmetic nature. Probably very few procedures would be withdrawn. Other than removal of tattoos what is there?

1 Harrison S, Hunter DJ, Johnstone I, Nicholson N, Thornhurst C, Wistow G. Health before health care. London: Institute for Public Policy Research, 1991.
2 Griffiths R. Community care. Agenda for action, London: HMSO, 1988.
3 Secretaries of State for Health, Social Security, Wales, and Scotland. Caring for people, community care in the next decade and beyond. London: HMSO, 1989. (Cmnd 849.)
4 Secretary of State for Health. The health of the nation. London: HMSO, 1991. (Cm 1523.)

An unfinished story

RUDOLF KLEIN, *professor, Centre for the Analysis of Social Policy, University of Bath*

Assessment of need

I am not convinced that we are very much better at assessing need than in 1974, when health authorities were first given responsibility for this; present day rhetoric is very much an echo of what Keith Joseph said when introducing his changes in the NHS. There is no technological fix. I am extremely sceptical about QALYs (quality adjusted life years). We don't have enough information about outcomes over time; costings are often poor; QALY calculations are very sensitive to the assumptions built into them; and categories of patients may be heterogeneous, so that what is cost effective for one patient may not necessarily be so for another. In any case, while QALYs may potentially be useful in helping us to choose between different priorities, this is very different from trying to build up an aggregate picture of need.

Standards in the NHS

Over the next few years, however, some of the information required to build up need assessments may start to emerge. The great advantage of the purchaser-provider split is that it forces things into the open: the implicit is gradually starting to become explicit as purchasing agreements and contracts are drawn up. We will start to know more about access to services, what is being done for whom, the measurement of standards, and whether defined standards are being held constant. So we might even be able to answer the question of whether standards in the NHS are falling or rising — which we cannot do at present.

Effectiveness of treatment

Measurement of the incidence of conditions has to be put together with consideration of the effectiveness of treatment for those conditions. There may be multiple options for treatment, some of which may take policy beyond the conventional limits of the NHS: that is to say, we may have to look at the competing claims of medical and social intervention. In the case of some chronic conditions — for example, osteoarthritis — making life more tolerable is a key priority, and it does not necessarily follow that putting more emphasis on such conditions will call for increased spending on medical intervention.

Funding

The arguments currently advanced for increases in the revenue spending on the NHS are unconvincing. The fact that other countries spend a higher proportion of their national income on health care, for example, does not tell us how much we ought to be spending on the NHS. It could simply be that they have higher unit costs, or that they spend more on ineffective procedures. In any case, the government is probably right that there is still scope for efficiency savings; consider, for example, the vast differences in prices charged for extracontractual referrals.

The argument is rather different when it comes to capital spending. We should be thinking about the kind of health care system that is likely to emerge over the next 20 years or so, and investing in a programme of modernisation. We know, for example, that there will be fewer women in the labour force; we may, furthermore, be trying to move from a low to a high wage economy; lastly, it is clear that the division of labour between primary and secondary health care is in the process of changing, perhaps radically. I would have thought that all this would imply a very different pattern of organisation. We need to review the whole nature of hospital provision. It may be that, as in the United States, there should be increasing emphasis on smaller community hospitals. We may have to invest more in labour saving technology. And so on. Working out a programme of modernisation, and arguing for more investment to support it, might be seen as a more constructive approach than extrapolating historical trends of expenditure or comparing Britain with other countries. In any case, any claim for extra money should be accompanied by a statement of what the extra funds will buy and for whom.

151

Insurance

It isn't self evident that any move from funding health care out of general taxation to a system of social insurance would necessarily mean extra money for the NHS. Governments worry about the level of insurance contributions in much the same way as they worry about the level of taxes, and try to keep them down — witness the examples of France and Germany. Moreover, there remains the problem of funding health care for those who cannot afford to fund it through an insurance system. So even with a social insurance system there would still be a large element of public expenditure, after all, even in the United States, 40% of all spending on health care comes from the government (and that is not counting tax expenditures — that is, tax concessions — which subsidise private insurance schemes). And we also know that these types of schemes tend to be expensive administratively and involve quite a lot of bureaucratic regulation.

Other options

There are obviously other policy options, which might help to tap people's apparent willingness to pay more for health care (as distinct from their general unwillingness to pay higher taxes). For example, a hypothecated health tax is often put forward as a candidate. But the trouble is that tax yields can fall as well as rise with changing economic circumstances. And while the Treasury remains as powerful as it is today it is likely to continue to have a strong influence on tax levels — hypothecated or not. The real difficulty, it seems to me, is that decisions about spending in a national system like the NHS are inescapably political, and there is no real way of getting round this short of dismantling it.

I am, however, attracted to the notion of raising at least some money for health care through local taxation. Thus it is possible to conceive of a system in which national taxation would fund the core NHS services, while local taxation would fund the rest. This would encourage public debate about priorities, create a sense of local ownership, and perhaps strengthen accountability to the community. It might be a particularly attractive option if health authorities were also to provide community care and social services: it isn't at all clear that local authorities have the managerial expertise required to carry out their new purchasing responsibilities. The case for this rests, however, less on the prospect of generating extra funds than on more general arguments for decentralisation and the acceptance of diversity. As the whole rumpus about local taxation in the 1980s has shown, the Treasury does not easily abdicate control over spending. It would almost certainly insist on capping the amount of money that could be raised.

Models of planning

The 1989 reforms represented, in one respect, the apotheosis of the top down rational planning model first introduced in 1974. The whole idea is that the purchasing authorities will define the needs of their populations and plan services accordingly. But I am sceptical about their capacity to do so. The technical tools are simply not sophisticated enough; moreover, if we assume that this neither can nor should be an exclusively technical process, there is the problem of a democractic deficit — the new health authorities lack political legitimacy. Given the lack of information and knowledge, the rational model may therefore be irrational in practice.

This is why, of course, the general practitioner fundholding experiment is so interesting. Initially I thought that this was a crackpot notion. I was wrong. It may well be that the conflict of perceptions and priorities between the top down view and the bottom up view exemplified by general practitioner fundholders will turn out to be a good thing. General practitioners are probably informed enough to be good purchasers for their patients; they are certainly better informed than the consumers themselves. And the fundholding system gives general practitioners incentives to inform themselves better about the effectiveness of different forms of treatment and their opportunity costs.

There remains a fundamental incompatibility between top down need planning and the diffusion of purchasing responsibility among fundholding general practitioners. Similarly, it is difficult to reconcile the fundholding model with accountability for the achievement of nationally determined targets. So this is very much an unfinished story, and we still have to see how the unresolved tensions between the two models work themselves out in the new NHS.

Working towards large health benefits

CHARLES NORMAND, *professor of health policy, London School of Hygiene and Tropical Medicine*

Assessment of need

Needs assessment will tell us a lot about the problems but will not necessarily solve them. It is important to think of the scale of the solutions, as priority should be given to large solutions, and not necessarily to partial solutions to large problems. We should perhaps concentrate effort on the margins, where there is more flexibility. How will a bit more or a bit less of a particular treatment modify the quality of outcomes and cost effectiveness?

There is a need to understand what the margins look like — that is, what is rock solid legitimate treatment and what is marginal? This should be a key area on the NHS research agenda. The problem is that the margins are often where the more interesting and dramatic treatments and advances lie, so there is often a perverse incentive to concentrate development where gains are small. There must be full and open debate on these matters so that proper prioritisation can be made.

Funding

Debate about funding of health is unsophisticated at present. More could be made of the apparent willingness of the population (expressed through opinion polls) to spend more on health. In some countries a large percentage of the health contribution or social services contribution, or both, comes from payroll tax — that is, through "insurance" paid for by employers, sometimes with a contribution from employees (for example, National Insurance). With such a system, however, there must be a mechanism for the government to pay the contribution for the poor, elderly, and

154

socially disadvantaged people who cannot pay their own contribution. The advantage of this system is the visibility of the funding of health services.

Arguments on funding relating to the percentage of the gross domestic product spent on health are not strong for various reasons. In reality, the percentage spent is tied most closely with the pay scales of those employed by the service and other input costs. (Incidentally, I believe that the percentage of the gross domestic product spent on health in the United Kingdom will rise as a result of capital charging — that is, increasingly money will be spent on "renting" buildings.) The important thing in assessing funding needs is to work on the potential benefits that are being forgone elsewhere in the economy which would increase quality of life (for example, by return of useful employment, etc). Perhaps this need can be assessed in the acute sector, but I am worried that there may appear to be a bottomless pit of apparently useful spending when assessing the needs of the chronically ill and those being cared for in the community.

Prioritisation

The Oregon approach has to be seen in the United States context. It is highly relevant when there is a significant poverty trap — a non-insured part of the population. It has been useful in encouraging public discussion on priorities but has taken a great deal of time and effort to develop and can only really deal with the issues rather superficially at present.

Prevention

The efficacy of many prevention programmes is often unproved. A lot of schemes being promoted in general practice at present cannot be shown to be cost effective. Therefore investment in screening programmes must be analysed very carefully. Primary prevention programmes (lifestyle) may lead to a demonstrable gain in health, but I have doubts about many secondary prevention programmes; my main concern is about the parity of evidence.

Health market

I believe that the purchaser-provider concept is reasonable, but the system whereby chinese walls have been set up within health authorities to separate their purchasing and providing roles needs to be reviewed. I am a strong believer in the resource management initiative, which I think is a more fundamental reform — with its devolving of financial control down to individual hospital providers — than some of those introduced in the NHS and Community Care Act. Clinical directorates do direct work, direct control of resources, encourage prioritisation; medical audit will only improve the process of increasing medical accountability and responsibility.

Some of the bureaucratic problems in the contract system have got to be sorted out. I know of one self governing hospital where 5% of the income is from extracontractual referrals but 50% of management time is spent in negotiating and dealing with the problems connected with them. Also, the dividing line between emergency cases and non-emergency cases creates an enormous loophole which will be extremely difficult to police.

I see the structural anomalies in the new system being directly managed units and fundholding practices. I can see family health services authorities becoming prime purchasers, acting on behalf of general practitioner cooperatives.

Community care

Griffiths's proposals are right, but the government's response is wrong, particularly in relation to mental health services. Contrary to current thinking, I believe that there should be increasing but different medical involvement in the care of the mentally handicapped. Many of these patients also have psychiatric illnesses which need medical help, such as depressions and neuroses. Also, certain illnesses are more common in mentally handicapped people, so they have general medical needs as well. What is the role of psychiatrists for those with continuing care needs? Should control of mental illness remain with district health authorities? I strongly believe on the basis of good evidence that most of the "cardboard city" people with no fixed abode are not generally those who have been discharged from long stay hospitals but people with alcohol and drug problems or patients with recurrent acute psychiatric problems.

Towards effective health care

IAN RUSSELL, *director, Health Services Research Unit, University of Aberdeen*

Effectiveness and need

I believe that the NHS should now focus on providing *effective* health care; I mean care that improves the health or welfare of patients. Whenever possible evidence about effectiveness should be sought through rigorous evaluation. In Aberdeen, for example, we are currently undertaking randomised trials to evaluate a wide range of unproved techniques, including hysteroscopic surgery and bone scanning to screen for osteoporosis. But in the absence of trials the NHS will have to use other evidence about effectiveness. Take the example of computed tomography: although the spread of computed tomographic scanning was based on only one randomised trial, there is a lot of evidence that it has enhanced diagnostic accuracy; but there is little evidence that it has changed the natural history of disease.

So the NHS will often have to fall back on professional consensus. Consensus conferences are an attractive way of sifting the available evidence, because they are both public and explicit. These conferences are very popular in the United States. Those organised by the King's Fund in this country have tried to achieve consensus across a wide range of interests, for both professional people and lay people. Consensus guidelines for health care will be needed for the foreseeable future; they can fill the gaps in our scientific knowledge and also identify where research should be targeted in future.

How does the concept of "need" relate to effectiveness? I am sure that need should be assessed only on the basis of effective care; patients cannot need care that does not improve their health or welfare. So health services research should concentrate on the evaluation of effectiveness, rather than the assessment of total need. Too much current work to assess need has lost sight of the goal of "health gain."

157

Setting priorities

Even if the health care purchased could be limited to that known to be effective, choices would be necessary. I would prefer to purchase those forms of health care that generate the largest "health gain" per pound spent. To achieve this the NHS needs more information on the true costs of health care and a general measure of health gain that could be used, for example, to compare heart transplant operations with hip replacements. A lot of work is still needed to improve the quality adjusted life year (QALY) as a general measure of health gain, but a league table of "best buys" in health care would be a great help in setting priorities.

Such a league table has three dangers. Firstly, there is the danger that forms of health care for which benefits and costs are easily quantified will dominate those with less tangible effects. Secondly, the setting of local priorities must reflect local circumstances as well as national league tables. Thirdly, and most importantly, these league tables must be open to public debate. In other words, the NHS should provide care that is equitable as well as effective.

Achieving effectiveness

How can effectiveness and equity be put into practice? I think the purchaser-provider principle is basically sound. Although I was disappointed that many of the initial contracts were little more than gentlemen's agreements, it would have been difficult to do better in such a short time. To avoid fudges in future we need much better information, especially about effectiveness

The main responsibility for providing this information lies with the NHS director of research and development. I applaud the decisions to publish an effectiveness bulletin and set up a clearing house for measuring patient outcomes — that is, health gain. But it is even more important to set up a centre to commission and coordinate overviews of all the available scientific evidence on the effectiveness of a wide range of clinical procedures.

The NHS must ensure that procedures known to be effective are used effectively in clinical practice. I am keen that clinical audit should be used for this role. If clinical audit is to improve health care, incentives are needed. While incentives to take part in audit would be a good first step, incentives to keep to clinical guidelines are even more important. Ideally these guidelines should be based on rigorous evaluation, but, as I mentioned before, consensus guidelines will be needed for the foreseeable future.

As both contracts and clinical audit have the potential to improve health care, they should be linked in future. In Scotland the Clinical Resource and Audit Group provides a useful forum for advancing both effectiveness on the one hand and professional audit on the other. The group is chaired by the chief medical officer for Scotland and includes representatives of the Scottish Office, health service management, and the health professions. I hope that an analogous body within each English region would prove equally effective, but I doubt whether there is sufficient expertise at district level.

Research and development

I would argue that health professionals also need incentives to introduce new forms of health care. The research and development budget should fund multicentre trials to evaluate these innovations, and also subsidise the purchase of the necessary equipment and the direct costs of the new service. As the NHS as a whole will benefit from a successful trial that provides evidence of effectiveness, the NHS, not the individual health districts, should pay for that trial.

There is merit in building a commitment to research and development into the contracts of a wide range of health professionals. I accept that doctors in teaching hospitals have more experience of research, and perhaps more scientific curiosity, but my experience in Scotland over the past five years suggests that other hospitals and other professionals can make a major contribution to the evaluation of health both care, old and new.

Funding

I believe that the NHS needs new investment if it is to become more effective. I see a strong case for bringing the level of funding in England and Wales up to that in Scotland. In my experience the higher level of funding in Scotland is reflected in higher staff morale and greater public satisfaction. Suppose the resulting dividend for England and Wales were estimated at 10 per cent, taking account of national differences in morbidity and so on. This increase in investment should be phased in over, say, 10 years. Priorities could then be carefully assessed against the new criteria of effectiveness and equity rather than the old criterion of expediency.

Conclusion

I hope that in 10 years' time health services researchers will have done enough work on the health gains and costs of different types of care to yield a comprehensive league table of health care priorities. Although the "best buys" could then be purchased without much argument, the choice between activities lower in the list of priorities would be the subject of well informed public debate. Purchasers would at last be able to buy health care, confident about the likely health gains, the likely costs, and the degree of public support. In short, the NHS must now aim to make more effective decisions, leading to more effective health care.

Resource management: need for a definition

MARTIN BUXTON, *professor, Health Economics Research Group, Brunel University*

Accountability

As one of the key issues for the health service is how much is spent in a given year, the management of the service just cannot be totally divorced from the secretary of state. The NHS Management Executive is being sent to Leeds to show that there is a clear distinction, but I have doubts about how this will work.

The idea is that when the system begins to work locally, central politicians will have only to push policy priorities from above, leaving the detail to local management. Neighbouring district health authorities, however, provide different patterns of care both in content and quality; it is precisely these differences that often become political issues so, in the end, politicians will find it hard to keep their distance.

Prioritisation

The BMA has to consider what the public can reasonably expect the NHS to provide. We should encourage a public debate on what should be available to all.

Other than tattoos and some cosmetic surgical services, should injuries or conditions which are "self inflicted" be funded within a health service — for instance, sports injuries? Should the smoker have the same rights to care as the non-smoker who gets lung cancer? In the insurance world good behaviour helps — for example, premiums are reduced if burglar alarms are installed and if a burglary takes place when the house was not locked cover may be lost. In insurance based systems such decisions have to be made. In Holland, for example, heart transplant operations are available as it has been decided that they are cost effective, whereas liver transplant operations are not yet routinely available.

Rationing

In relation to rationing, I believe that the excitement over waiting lists is all rather false. One way of determining priority, as far as patients are concerned, would be to ask them how much money they would require to take their names off the waiting list. Granted, if they were given money they could use it to buy their treatment in the private sector, but the real point is to assess priority and to find out what value patients put on resolving their condition.

I approve of the approach being used in places like Oregon in principle because, again, the information provided will indicate the value that people put on different types of care or "health state changes." I'm concerned, however, that the Oregon approach is superficial and does not take into account the real costs involved. One thing that might be achieved by this sort of work is a demonstration of how misinformed the public are and, if the surveyors are not careful, the work could actually perpetuate the misunderstandings.

In relation to cancer treatment the public may want only the treatments which are of proved effectiveness — that is, those that increase the quantity or quality of life — which could be inflexible in relation to development work.

Need

I do not like the concept of a bottomless pit of need. I prefer the model of there being a topless supply of ingenuity by the medical profession with the boundaries constantly receding at the top while need is, possibly, fairly constant at the bottom.

Funding

I agree that health in the United Kingdom is less well funded than in other countries but cannot go on to argue that the answer is just to fund it at a higher level. I believe that the service just cannot do all that the people think it should do, although I'm not sure that the current arrangements for distributing finance to government departments adequately reflect public priorities.

A link with the Organisation for Economic Co-operation and Development (OECD) average level of spending on health care, for instance, would take control from the Treasury, but would it actually be any better? Even a hypothecated health tax would still, inevitably, be dominated by the Treasury.

I am against an insurance system for producing extra funding. Could a purchasing authority say that, for instance, the standard cost for a patient's hernia repair is £400 and give patients a £400 voucher, enabling them to top up and buy extra facilities if they wish or speed up their care by going to the private sector? Should patients be able to pay to jump the queue in this way?

Private sector

Is the BMA considering the position of consultants who work in both the NHS and the private sector? I have a real concern that there may be abuse of the system. It will be vital for managers to know and monitor the facts; I think that there must be clear individual contracts which include accountability, fixed sessions, and some indication of what type of patients are being cared for and how many. The profession must work to decrease the possibility of abuse of the system or the issue will remain as a black cloud and part of the mystique of the in效fficiency of the NHS.

Hospital services

I'm sure that there are inefficiencies in many areas of the hospital service, but often through imposed constraints. For instance, when planning hospitals the planners are not allowed to make mistakes, so the whole process seems to go on for ever; another constraint is the reluctance of politicians ever to sanction closures.

I have been closely involved with the resource management initiative because of the work of Brunel University. I'm quite positive about the increasing development of clinical directorates. I have seen that the approach can work. I'm only sorry that it took so long to demonstrate. The information side, however, is more of a problem. The a priori assumption is that "with better information we can all make better decisions," but often the distinction has not been drawn between data and information.

It has to be accepted that decisions may often be easier when the figures are produced on a piece of paper rather than by using complicated data turned out by modern information technology. Therefore, there is a need for simple information, much of which is

163

already available; the real question relates to what type of complex information is needed.

It has been difficult to analyse the formal resource management initiative because it was hijacked by the reforms. The later sites, however, were set up in the contracting situation, so they are beginning to adapt to the purchaser-provider concept. One of the problems has been that there has not been a real definition of resource management. I believe that at subunit level resource management is compatible with contracting in that it should help with clinical contract management, but now, because hospitals are not having to make all their own priority decisions because the purchasers are meant to be deciding what they provide, at least part of the original resource management loop is likely to be taking place outside the hospital.

Purchaser-provider concept

I believe that the general concept of the purchaser-provider system is sensible, but I'm sure that health authority purchasers and fundholder purchasers are incompatible; I think there will soon be evidence appearing that this is the case. The government should have tested both models — that is, primary purchasing through fundholders and primary purchasing through district health authorities. Now we have such a variety of models that it would be difficult to do comparative assessment.

An insurance based system

DAVID GREEN, *director Health and Welfare Unit, Institute of Economic Affairs*

Insurance

The assessment of need approach to funding is too technical; it allows too much discretion to professionals. Indeed, I believe that a needs assessment approach like QALYs (quality adjusted life years) is immoral because the allocation of health care services cannot be put on to a rigidly technical footing.

I would start from a different base altogether. It is a question of who has the responsibility to be cost conscious. If it is the provider then the provider gains too much power, whereas if it is the patient then the patient has control of his or her own destiny. An insurance based health care system puts the purchaser of insurance in a position to make choices about the range of services and style of medical practice they are prepared to pay for.

I accept that in the United States the system has serious flaws, but these are the result of imprudent government interventions, not failures of the market as such. There are three problems: firstly, because many people are insured by their employers, their insurance is, in effect, free and they have no motivation to be cost conscious; secondly, huge open ended tax subsidies for health insurance; and, thirdly, state laws which mandate what care has to be covered, so it is not possible to offer a cheap no frills insurance policy to those not insured. The problem in the United States is that there is not a proper market because it has been wrecked by imprudent government intervention.

In my paper entitled "Everyone a private patient" I advocated the right for people to contract out of the NHS.[1] Instead they would be able to claim a voucher — the value of which would be worked out on the basis of age — and then spend the voucher on insurance;

165

obviously they could add more if they wished. Therefore, if patients do not like the NHS they will opt out but if they prefer it then they will continue to use it; if too many opted out then the NHS would have to improve or it would fail.

Competition

I'm convinced that the best type of professionalism is encouraged by competition. Markets reinforce the professional ethos of service by rewarding those providers who please their patients. I accept that many patients will accept whatever they are offered without challenge, but it takes only a few vigorous people to make markets work. Doctors should be able to sell their skills more openly through advertising to encourage them to serve their patients and to set free the spirit of innovation and creativity in service provision which a monopoly suppresses. Progress occurs in a competitive market because the worst providers must emulate the best or go out of business.

I believe that, as well as competition between doctors, there will be competition between insurers. I think that an insurance dominated market could contain costs without interfering too much with professional judgment, although there would need to be checks such as prehospital admission authorisations. I know that insurance based systems are expensive, but German and French hospitals, for instance, are generally better than ours and have very few waiting lists. The principal reason for the difference between spending on health in the United States and Canada is the very different age structure in the two countries. The United States would be a good insurance model to follow if the government and states had not wrecked the market by their interventions.

Fundholding

I accept that there were some benefits in the NHS model before the reforms; the general practitioner, for instance, had open access to secondary care with no explicit cash limits. I believe that fundholding has the potential to destroy the doctor-patient relationship, in which I am a strong believer. The patient now not only goes to seek health care but also to ask the general practitioner whether he or she can have a share of the public purse; quite apart from its effects on the doctor-patient relationship this is undesirable because the patient is put in a weak position. There is a need for cost consciousness, but it should result from consumers being cost conscious on their own behalf, not the political and medical authorities in the interests of "efficiency."

1 Green D. *Everyone a private patient*. London: Institute of Economic Affairs, 1988.

Putting a better case to the Treasury

ALAN MAYNARD, *professor*, *Centre for Health Economics, University of York*

Assessment of need

If "need" is defined as the patient's ability to benefit from care and the NHS is to meet the needs of the population, cost effectiveness must be analysed to identify the least expensive way of improving health. Those who allocate resources, be they purchasers or providers, have to identify the marginal health benefits of alternative treatments competing for funds.

Though most treatments are of unknown cost and effect, there is much information on effectiveness and cost effectiveness that is unused. The design and results of clinical and economic trials should be appraised critically and continuously, with the results of well conducted studies being identified and disseminated systematically. The American work on outcomes is as limited as that in the United Kingdom, with poor linkage of mortality records and inefficient use of available health related quality of life instruments. Much research and the work of the royal colleges on medical audit is inappropriately focused, emphasising limited clinical end points rather than issues relevant to purchasers and providers — that is, the cost effectiveness of competing treatments.

Research

The reorganisation of NHS research and development is fraught with difficulties, not only in the design of evaluative studies but also in the definition of health services research. The focus of clinical research is the individual patient and the appropriate design of clinical trials is the random controlled trial. In health services research the focus is the delivery of care and the institutional and budgetary context in which is takes place. Health services research has no gold standard approach, is rarely carried out in a systematic experiment, and uses statistical techniques to detect relationships, rather like epidemiologists seek to identify risk factors. Obviously, health services research and clinical research can be complementary.

The new chief of NHS research and development, Michael Peckham, is developing a national strategy with a top down and, as yet, ill defined management structure. Enhanced ringfenced funding and a system of support to create and develop research careers are necessary ingredients in this process. However, most of all the narrow clinical research approach must be abandoned and health services research developed to inform purchaser and provider choices.

Resource allocation

The funding of the NHS by formulas such as those of the Resource Allocation Working Party (RAWP) in England is related to population and need, proxied by standardised mortality ratios. The use of standardised mortality ratios rewards those regions that kill more of their population! Funding should be targeted at *avoidable* mortality and morbidity.

Weighting population measures by morbidity (using the first health and lifestyles survey) rather than standardised mortality ratios has a significant effect on the regional distribution of NHS funding.[1] The available data to reflect deprivation are inadequate and produce inadequate measures (such as the Jarman index). There is a need not only for more and better epidemiology but also for the training of a cadre of clinical epidemiologists (as at McMaster University, Canada) who could work in conjunction with economists "picking apart" the design and content of evaluative studies.

Progress in measurement, both in terms of quality and quantity, will be slow, but the NHS reforms offer the medical profession and researchers a real opportunity to develop evaluative science and health services research. Perhaps in time the chief medical officer, the chief of research and development, and the Department of Health will support research in this way in order to inject into the annual round of public expenditure planning better information to sustain the case put to the Treasury to increase NHS funding. At present the Department of Health's cases are supported by miscellaneous guesses (for example, about the impacts of the aging of the population) and mutually agreed myths (for example, about the effects of new technology on annual funding).

Structure

At the local level general practitioner fundholding practices may be too small to carry their population's risks. The failure to create sensible reporting systems, not just for finance but for epidemiological purposes, is unfortunate. To carry risks fundholders may have to form clubs, either formally or informally, and, in so doing, reinvent the family health services authority or district health authority purchaser structure. The developments in primary care have been poorly evaluated and not thought through systematically: structural reform has been determined by the limited products of doodles on the back of envelopes.

In the hospital sector the purchaser-provider divide may create changes that induce efficiency. However, this needs evaluation, and the same effects could possibly have been achieved by less radical reforms that ensured that money followed the patients more efficiently.

Both the resource management initiative and clinical directorates are generic terms that have been developed in various ways at the local level. The evaluation of the resource management initiative (by the Brunel research group) shows disappointingly few returns to a large investment.[2] Clinical directorates, like the resource management initiative, need continuous evaluation too. The investment in information technology during the reforms has been large, with no central coordination to agree either core data requirements or the identification of a few suppliers, who could have then exploited economics of scale and offered hardware at a lower unit price. Much money has been wasted on useless kit which fails not only to provide often ill defined local data needs but also to provide integrated, communicating data systems at the local and national level.

Accountability

The ministers will continue to be accountable for the NHS budget, and it is possible that the NHS Management Executive's move to Leeds is already doomed. Ministers need to be made more accountable. They react to criticism and "crises" by enunciating more "priorities." Over the past decade there have been a large number of crises and priorities. This nonsense process begs many questions. By what decision making process are these priorities made? How are the priorities ranked? What funding is available for them? — There are no answers. Ministers have devalued the word "priority" to such an extent it is meaningless.

The region review process, by which ministers visited and questioned regional health authorities, seems to have lost momentum. The select committee might usefully appraise what regions have been asked to do and how well action has been defined, as well as the extent to which change has been induced.

Prevention

The approach that produced *The Health of Nation*[3] was informed by the 1989 paper on health targets of the New Zealand Labour government.[4] The central issue in prevention and its public debate is the target — are targets to be definite causes of death (for example, cardiovascular disease) or risk factors (such as alcohol and tobacco use)? Targeting risk factors seems more sensible, and by far the most important avoidable risk factor is tobacco. The Conservative party now seems less resistant to this approach than it was when under the previous regime, and it or a Labour government might move towards banning tobacco advertisements by initially levying a 100% tax on advertising revenue, which would be earmarked to fund anti-tobacco advertisements. The BMA and researchers need to continue to focus attention on the control of tobacco and explore the extent to which risk factors such as drinking alcohol can also be reduced.

Conclusion

Progress on evaluation, resource allocation, and prevention requires multidisciplinary collaboration between the BMA, the royal colleges, and researchers. This could and should be improved and could facilitate the enhancement of the health of the population.

1 Carr-Hill R. A., Maynard A., Slack R. *Morbidity Variation and RAWP. J. Epidemiol Community Health* 1990; **44**: 271–3.
2 Packwood T, Keen J, Buxton M. *Hospitals in transition: the resource management experiment.* London: Open University Press, 1991.
3 Secretary of State for Health. *The health of the nation.* London: HMSO, 1991. (Cm 1523.)
4 Ministry of Health. *New Zealand health goals and targets.* Wellington: MoH, 1989.

More choices for patients

ROBERT MAXWELL, *chief executive, King's Fund*

Funding

I believe that the traditional model of central allocation of funds has the benefit of simplicity; it is strong on control and encourages thinking in a "cash envelope." From the '50s to the '70s, when there was a comparative boom in health finance, central rationing was good because the main danger (evidenced in many health systems) was one of extravagance. The weaknesses of the system may, however, get worse in the future as the workload increases faster than the funding and the population increases in age. Central rationing will continue to be the controlling influence, but the system is crude and is unlikely to be responsive to patient or professional requirements. Will it, therefore, be an adequate mechanism in the future?

I am suspicious of assessment of need as a platform for funding. It suggests that need is a firm and absolute concept, which it is not. The purchaser-provider concept is good in so far as it will encourage an attempt to understand the needs of the local population. Health care, however, depends on how much the purchaser can afford to spend, so rather than assessing need in an abstract way it is more sensible to start with a pretty clear notion of what you can afford before considering how to get the best value for that money.

Prioritisation

We cannot afford to ignore the private sector in relation to its activity or to consumer demand. The private sector's capacity to deliver should be exploited, but I'm concerned about any major slide towards the private sector, which could destabilise the idea of the state system.

172

Prioritisation will be a central theme for the next 10-20 years, during which time medicine will continue to develop and the developments will, usually, not be money saving. Indeed, although people will live longer they will inevitably die of something else, possibly something more expensive.

No country is good at prioritisation. The United Kingdom has not done a bad job in relation to other countries. It has a strong primary care system with a gatekeeper role and the hardest decisions are communicated to patients by doctors in a humane way. Would bureaucratic rules serve patients any better?

How can we do better? Firstly, we can continue to root out waste throughout the NHS — for instance, through efficiency drives and monitoring of general practitioner prescribing. Secondly, more work can be done to provide evidence of effectiveness of treatments; this should include work on the quality of life for patients after treatment and would have a knock on effect on general practitioner referral patterns.

I believe in medical or clinical audit, not just because the government supports it but because it will enable professionals and patients to make better choices. The government should be prepared to ventilate the real issues relating to choice nationally to encourage a public debate — this would be better than focusing on precise scales of local priorities (as in the Oregon approach).

Purchaser-provider concept

There has been a tradition in the United Kingdom of doctors doing the best they can for the patient in front of them with little regard to the "rules" and at the same time rationing the available care. This compromise is not always bad for the patient but it conceals inefficiencies and painful choices. At least in an insurance system the buyers or patients have the chance to make their own priorities. The purchaser-provider concept may lead to more open dialogue on these matters and to a better focus on the choices available. In that sense the concept is a welcome shift towards attempting to get the best for the population.

Models

Purchasing at present has the two elements of district health authorities and fundholders. This is a compromise that lacks coherence. The purchaser should either be the district health

173

authority, or the general practitioner budget holder, or, alternatively, the sort of health maintenance organisation originally envisaged by Enthoven in America. A weakness of the district health authority as purchaser is that the consumer has little choice — it is not as easy to move district as it is to change general practitioner. District health authorities are now merging, which will give them even larger populations and make them even less locally accountable. Nevertheless, the different models are part of a healthy experiment that will probably continue for some considerable time. I simply do not see both types of purchasing as viable in the long term.

Accountability

The current local authority system is a strong model because local authority members are elected locally and a significant part of local authority funding is raised locally. In this regard, the Institute for Public Policy Research (IPPR) model of unitary local authorities "commissioning" health care is less strong as, presumably, most of the money will be awarded by bloc grant from central government.

Regional government is more locally accountable in Scotland, Wales, and Northern Ireland than in England. In Canada central government calls the strategic shots by laying down rules on local entitlement and by encouraging health promotion, for instance, but stands well back from more operational matters. In England the Canadian model could develop, at least in part, through greater devolution of executive power to regional health authorities through the NHS Management Executive.

Community care

I believe that the proposal of the second Griffiths report[1] to move more towards a case management function in the community are sensible in that they might encourage local authority and health authority funds to be used in compatible ways. This cannot work, however, if either side is starved of funds. At present social services departments are clearly having appreciable financial problems and, with no sign of this improving, there must be a large question mark over the implementation of *Caring for People*.[2]

There is a need for better synergy between social services case management and general practitioners. People have more respect for general practitioners than for the social services but, for work-load reasons alone, general practitioners probably could not be case managers. Nevertheless, they must continue to act as patients' advocates in relation to their care in the community.

1 Griffiths R. *Community care: agenda for action*. London: HMSO, 1988.
2 Secretaries of State for Health, Social Security, Wales, and Scotland. *Caring for people, community care in the next decade and beyond*. London: HMSO, 1989. (Cmnd 849.)

An American perspective

DONALD W LIGHT, *professor of health services and policy, University of Medicine and Dentistry of New Jersey*

Starting point

Assessment of health needs in coming years into the twenty first century is crucial. What are the implications, for instance, of the increase in the number of elderly people in the population and the greater emphasis on health promotion and prevention of illness? How will the health service have to change to cope with these needs in terms of provision, financial arrangements, and delivery structure?

It is macho for doctors to see themselves to be at the "cutting edge," but there is also a need to understand and promote methods of medical excellence which do not always rely solely on the latest scientific techniques. There is much more to good medicine than high technology; focusing on listening skills and communication techniques, for instance, could in itself have economic and public relations implications. These skills are very important as the economic pressures presented by the NHS reforms erode doctor-patient trust; there should be as little financial threat to the doctor-patient relationship as possible.

Health insurance

Private insurance in the United Kingdom tends to pick off the easier, cheaper treatments. I suggest that the Canadian law be adopted, prohibiting private insurance from covering services provided by the national system — that is, to avoid a two tier service and inequity.

We must decide whether we want private medicine at higher fees for corporate employees and privileged citizens and public medicine

176

in run down facilities on the cheap for the rest. Private insurance always costs more. In the United States the perk of private health insurance is now a major issue for employers. Tax relief for private insurance merely encourages the bifurcation even more.

The NHS is more cost effective than the private insurance sector. There is a need to capitalise on the patients' willingness to pay more tax towards health. Could more be made of National Insurance contributions — that is, could they be put towards health and social services? (This would be difficult politically owing to problems in industry and small businesses.) An alternative could be a national earmarked health and social services tax.

Another model would be a core service provided through general taxation with money raised locally for "extra" facilities and services. This could encourage local discussion and debate on services and priorities (a mini-Oregon) and encourage community ownership. There could be a partnership with local industry. Contributions could be voluntary (direct or through a lottery) or compulsory through local taxation.

Purchaser-provider concept

There is little evidence that markets are beneficial to health care. They tend to drive costs up and increase both inequity and wastes.

Currently care in the United Kingdom is split with at least three different budget holders: health authorities control the budget for hospital care and community care; family health services authorities that for primary care; and local authorities that for community care.

Different budgets means constant disputes over whose budget will pay, for example, for prescribing and community care. A common approach would be more sensible.

To devolve budgets down to general practitioner fundholders makes matters worse. They will purchase only for their own panel without regard to the population at large, so planning provision will be almost impossible. The family health services authority or district health authority might be a better purchaser in line with the new social health maintenance organisation concept in the United States. These organisations purchase care (including community care) from birth to death, ideally on the basis of need; however, this requires a population of 0.25-0.5 million in order to plan sensibly.

If this approach were to be taken it could well change the culture and the nature of many hospitals. There would be a primary and

community care based system with hospitals providing back up —
that is, in many cases hospitals would probably become less high
tech and reduce in number. In such a system there would have to
be some accountability to the local population, perhaps through
"consumer advisory councils."

There is a need for consultants to be as responsive as general
practitioners to the needs of the population, so it would be crucial
that hospital consultants were directly involved in discussing such
changes. Purchasers should have advisory boards that include
epidemiologists, general practitioners, and practising clinicians to
encourage a realistic approach. This could lead to better response to
need and better integration of care. Consultants might consult in
the community and be prepared to allow suitably trained general
practitioners to do more hospital work — for instance, routine
minor surgical procedures which do not provide much satisfaction
for consultants.